JESUS,
THE GREAT
I AM

Stanford E. Murrell

Ichthus Publications · Apollo, Pennsylvania

Copyright © 2019 by Stanford E. Murrell

All rights reserved. No part of this publication may be reproduced, stored in a retrieval system, or transmitted, in any form or by any means, electronic, mechanical, photocopying, recording or otherwise, without prior permission of the publisher or the Copyright Licensing Agency.

Our goal is to provide high-quality, thought-provoking books that foster encouragement and spiritual growth. For more information regarding Ichthus Publications, other IP books, or bulk purchases, visit us online or write to support@ichthuspublications.com.

Unless otherwise indicated, all Scripture quotations are taken from the King James Version, public domain.

Printed in the United States of America

Jesus, The Great I Am
ISBN: 978-1-946971-52-4

www.ichthuspublications.com

Dedicated to the Memory and Teachings of

Dr. R. C. Sproul

1939–2017

Contents

Foreword *vii*

1	Jesus, Why Did You Come	13
2	A Day of Triumph	31
3	The Doctrine Jesus Taught	39
4	Jesus and His Transfiguration	45
5	I AM the Bread of Life	55
6	I AM the Light of the World	67
7	I AM the Door	75
8	I AM the Good Shepherd	83
9	I AM the Resurrection	95
10	I AM the Way, the Truth, and the Life	111
11	I AM the True Vine	125
12	The Eighth "I AM"	137

Foreword

While browsing through the books of a local Barnes and Noble in Melbourne, Florida, I became intrigued when I came across a work with the title, *The Great Philosophers: From Socrates to Foucault.* I have enjoyed reading this work, but was curiously surprised at the absence of Jesus of Nazareth being numbered among the "great philosophers," in light of the attempts to define philosophy. While the word philosophy literally means "love of wisdom," there is no broad based consensus of a working definition.

Some believe philosophy is best viewed in terms of abstract subject matter. It attempts to answer such questions as "What exists?" "How do we know?" "What are we going to do about it?" "Who am I?" Where did I come from?" Where am I going?" "How should I live my life?"

Others believe philosophy is best understood in terms of methodology. The method should be careful and systematic thinking, giving reasons for the conclusions, and allowing those conclusions to be focused. Anyone can give a reason for something being right or wrong, but the view becomes philosophy when it is rooted in reason.

There is a third view of philosophy. It is best understood as an attitude, or a way of life. Socrates, for example, died believing the unexamined life was not worth living. This understanding of philosophy stands in contrast, and sometimes conflicts, with a systematic methodology, or metaphysics and epistemology.

I would suggest, in Jesus Christ, all three of these approaches to philosophy converge, which is not surprising, for all truth is God's truth. Jesus said, "I am The Way, The Truth, and the Life" (John 14:6).

In light of this reality, the absence of Jesus listed among the greatest philosophers is not only highly peculiar, it renders the work manifestly deficient. As absurd as it would be to write a book on the history of the United States without ever mentioning George Washington, for example, it is even more bizarre not to chronicle the wisdom of Jesus in a book about wisdom.

Foreword

For those lovers of wisdom who lean towards metaphysics and epistemology, hear Christ, as He cries out, "I am come a light into the world, that whosoever believeth on me should not abide in darkness. And if any man hear my words, and believe not, I judge him not: for I came not to judge the world, but to save the world. He that rejecteth me, and receiveth not my words, hath one that judgeth him: the word that I have spoken, the same shall judge him in the last day. For I have not spoken of myself; but the Father which sent me, he gave me a commandment, what I should say, and what I should speak. And I know that his commandment is life everlasting: whatsoever I speak therefore, even as the Father said unto me, so I speak" (John 12:46–50).

For those lovers of wisdom who enjoy methodology, study the Sermon on the Mount in the Gospel of Matthew, chapters 5—7, and you will find a systematic way of thinking, with rational conclusions, for all that is articulated.

And for those who believe philosophy is best comprehended and understood in an attitude, or way of life, "Behold the Man." He has astonished multitudes.

Jesus, the Great I Am

The nineteenth century preacher James Allen Francis noted in his famous essay, "One Solitary Life",

> Here is a man who was born in an obscure village, the child of a peasant woman. He grew up in another obscure village. He worked in a carpenter shop until He was thirty, and then for three years He was an itinerant preacher. He never wrote a book. He never held an office. He never owned a home. He never set foot inside a big city. He never traveled two hundred miles from the place where He was born. He had no credentials but Himself.
>
> While still a young man, the tide of popular opinion turned against Him. His friends ran away. One of them denied Him. He was turned over to His enemies. He went through the mockery of a trial. He was nailed upon a cross between two thieves. His executioners gambled for the only piece of property He had on earth while He was dying—and that was His coat. When He was dead, He was taken down and laid in a borrowed grave through the pity of a friend.
>
> Nineteen wide centuries have come and gone, and today He is the centerpiece of the

human race, and the leader of progress. I am far within the mark when I say that all the armies that ever marched, and all the navies that ever were built, and all the parliaments that ever sat, and all the kings that ever reigned, put together, have not affected the life of man upon this earth as powerfully as that One Solitary Life.[1]

All the philosophies of life are united in Christ. All other philosophers are lesser luminaries of that One Solitary Life. Jesus alone stands as the great, "I AM."

To foster appreciation for the "I AM" statements of Jesus, the purpose of His coming, the celebration of His presence, the profound doctrine He taught, and the purposeful manifestation of His glory are briefly noted so that He might be praised.

> Be this, while life is mine,
> My song of love divine:
> > *May Jesus Christ be praised!*
> Sing this eternal song
> Through all the ages long:
> > *May Jesus Christ be praised!*

---

[1] As quoted in Josh McDowell, *Evidence that Demands a Verdict*.

1

Jesus, Why Did You Come?

"And it came to pass in those days, that there went out a decree from Caesar Augustus, that all the world should be taxed. (And this taxing was first made when Cyrenius was governor of Syria.) And all went to be taxed, every one into his own city. And Joseph also went up from Galilee, out of the city of Nazareth, into Judaea, unto the city of David, which is called Bethlehem; (because he was of the house and lineage of David) to be taxed with Mary his espoused wife, being great with child. And so it was, that, while they were there, the days were accomplished that she should be delivered. And she brought forth her firstborn son, and wrapped him in swaddling clothes, and laid him in a manger; because there was no room for them in the inn. And there were in the same country shepherds abiding in the field, keeping watch over their flock by night. And, lo, the angel of the Lord came upon them, and the glory of the Lord shone round about them: and they were sore afraid. And the angel said unto them, 'Fear not: for, behold, I bring you good tidings of great joy, which shall be to all people. For unto you is born this day in the city of David a Savior, which is Christ the Lord. And this shall be a sign unto you; ye shall find the babe wrapped in swaddling clothes, lying in a manger.' And suddenly there was with the angel a multitude of the heavenly host praising God, and saying, 'Glory to God in the highest, and on earth peace, good will toward men.' And it came to pass, as the angels were gone away from them into heaven, the shepherds said one to another, 'Let us now go even unto Bethlehem, and see this thing which is come to pass, which the Lord hath made known unto us.' And they came with haste, and found Mary, Joseph, and the babe lying in a manger. And when they had seen it, they made known abroad the saying which was told them concerning this child. And all they that heard it wondered at those things which were told them by the shepherds. But Mary kept all these things, and pondered them in her heart. And the shepherds returned, glorifying and praising God for all the things that they had heard and seen, as it was told unto them" (Luke 2:1–20).

In 1809, the international scene was filled with violence and turbulence. The French ruler Napoleon was marching through Austria; blood was flowing freely.

Despite the social carnage and political upheaval, important births were taking place. For example, William Gladstone was born that year. He was destined to become one of England's finest statesmen.

That same year in England, Alfred Lloyd Tennyson was born to a poor minister and his wife. The child would one day greatly affect the literary world in a marked manner.

On the American continent, the jurist and Supreme Court Justice Oliver Wendell Holmes was born in Cambridge, Massachusetts.

Not far away in Boston, a baby was born who would grow to be a poet and a writer of horror. Edgar Allan Poe began his eventful, albeit tragic, life.

It was also in that same year of 1809, that a physician in England named Darwin and his wife, named their child Charles Robert. He would one day go on a voyage aboard a ship named the *Beagle* and return to give the world his theory of evolution, the idea that all plants, animal, and man are descended from one common ancestor.

That same year produced the cries of a newborn infant in a rugged log cabin in Hardin County, Kentucky. The baby's name? Abraham Lincoln.

If there had been news broadcasts at that time, these words might have been heard: "The destiny of the world is being shaped on an Austrian battlefield today."

But history was actually being shaped away from the battlefields of Napoleon and his men in the cradles of England and America.

In like manner, the citizens thought taxation was the big news during the days of Caesar Augustus. But a young Jewish woman cradled the biggest news of all in her arms: the birth of the Savior.

Today, the gospel has captured the hearts of more than 2.2 billion people who profess to be Christian. As attention is turned to the Advent story, a fundamental question arises: "Jesus, why did you come?" The Bible records the answer.

First, the Bible teaches that Jesus Christ came to fulfill the promise God the Father made in the Covenant of Redemption. When Adam, acting as the Federal Representative of mankind, fell in the Garden of Eden, he condemned not only himself, but all of humanity to a godless state of existence. The Bible says, "Wherefore, as by one man sin entered into the world, and death by sin; and so death passed upon all men, for that all have sinned" (Romans 5:12).

Every person who is born into the world, is born with the plague of all plagues clinging to the soul, and permeating every fiber of existence. That plague is sin. What does sin do to self and others?

- Sin darkens the understanding.
- Sin perverts the emotions.
- Sin dominates the will.
- Sin moves men to love darkness rather than light.
- Sin creates chaos and confusion.
- Sin destroys the moral compass of the will while exalting pride, selfishness, and greed.
- Sin causes the body to burn with illicit desires, while trying to silence the conscience warning of a certain damnation.
- Sin defies God.

- Sin destroys relationships.
- Sin demands servitude and gives only death as wages in return.

Despite all the wars that have been waged, all the tears that have been shed, all the promises that have been made, all the self-loathing that has been expressed, the power of sin is still present.

Despite all the self-help programs on the market, despite all the professional counseling in the country, despite all the prisons that have been erected, despite all the personal shame that tormented souls carry in private, sin is still alive and well on planet earth.

Because sin is so pervasive and strong, if any soul is ever to know redemption and forgiveness of sins, then the question of sin must be confronted.

Because of infinite grace, in the same spot that sin was first conceived, God entered into a Covenant of Redemption with man.

God promised that one day Someone would come to reverse the works of unrighteousness, thereby allowing souls to be reconciled and have fellowship with the Sovereign, based upon the righteousness of justice satisfied. "Where sin abounded, grace did much more abound" (Romans 5:20).

The long wait for the fulfillment of the Covenant of Redemption began with great hopes and many expectations. But these expectations gave way to a patient waiting. During the waiting period, the Law came with all of its rituals and ceremonies. These rituals and rites served a purpose, which was to remind individuals that by the works of the Law no flesh can ever be justified in the sight of God. Moreover, the shedding of the blood of animals did not take away sin, for they were not perfect either, having been touched by the same plague that afflicts mankind.

Realizing this, religious men such as the Pharisees grew desperate. They hoped against hope that somehow the righteousness of God could be obtained by the blood of bulls and goats in association with many good works.

And yet, as David Clark noted, "Every smoking altar, every bleeding victim, every ascetic privation, every priestly intervention was a testimony to the guilt of sin, and the need of [a more perfect way for the] remission [of sins] . . ."

Lest mankind utterly despair, the prophets appeared to remind the people of the Prince who was to come, who would make a Covenant with His people. Finally, "in the fullness of time" (Galatians 4:4), at the appointed moment, the Messiah did appear suddenly in His holy temple. Later, He went and stood on the edge of the Jordan River to be baptized, in order to be presented as "the Lamb of God which taketh away the sin of the world" (John 1:29).

Upon hearing the Messiah had come, throngs of people in Palestine rushed to receive Christ, though others drew back. There were some who refused to believe that Jesus was the Anointed One. "But to as many as received Him, to them He gave the right to become the sons of God, even to as many as believed on His name" (John 1:12).

Tragically, there are still those who choose not to believe that Jesus is the Son of the Living God. They cannot believe that Christ is truly Emmanuel—God with us—despite abundant evidence that Jesus is who He claimed to be.

There is the evidence of the virgin birth, the influence of His personality upon the world, and the personal testimony of many. Regarding the Virgin Birth, it is a great mystery, but the Bible tells us that Jesus was born without personal sin, and without the imputation of Adam's sin.

How God could be both true deity and true humanity has occupied the conversation of theologians and Church Councils for centuries (Chalcedon A.D. 451). The Bible simply records the facts, without explanation, and calls upon the heart to believe in the miraculous because it is true.

The baby in the cradle of Bethlehem was also the Eternal Son, and as the Eternal Son, Jesus had something to say to the Father the night of His birth. And this is what Christ said when He came into the world: "Sacrifice and offering thou wouldest not, but a body hast thou prepared for me: In burnt offerings and sacrifices for sin Thou hast had no pleasure. Then said I, Lo, I come (in the volume of the book it is written of me), to do thy will, O God" (Hebrews 10:5–7).

Later, Roman historians would record that the world had been waiting for Someone as special as Jesus. Suetonius noted, "There had spread over all the Orient an old and established belief, that it was fated at that time for men coming from Judaea to rule the world" (Suetonius: *Life of Vespasian*, 4:5). Tacitus tells of the same expectation declaring "there was a firm persuasion . . . that at this very time the East was to grow powerful, and rulers coming from

Judaea were to acquire universal empire" (Tacitus: *Histories*, 5:13).

The Jews had hope "about that time, one from their country should become governor of the habitable earth" (Josephus: *Wars of the Jews*, 6:5, 4). In the fullness of time, God brought forth His Son (Galatians 4:4).

What a Son Jesus would prove to be. The totality of his life was a constant demonstration of His deity. By that life He became *The Man Who Changed the World*. Dr. Herbert Lockyer explains.

> More than 1,900 years ago there was a Man born contrary to the laws of life.
>
> This Man lived in poverty and was reared in obscurity.
>
> Only once did He cross the boundary of the country in which He lived: That was during His exile in childhood.
>
> In infancy He startled a king: in childhood,
>
> He puzzled the doctors: In manhood, He ruled the course of Nature, walked upon the billows as if pavement, and hushed the sea to sleep.
>
> He never wrote a book, and yet all of the libraries of the country could not hold the books that have been written about Him.

He never wrote a song, and yet He has furnished the theme for more songs than all the songwriters combined.

He never founded a college, but all the schools put together cannot boast of having as many students.

The names of the past, proved statesmen of Greece and Rome, have come and gone.

The names of past scientists, philosophers, and theologians, have come and gone; but the name of this Man abounds more and more.

Though time has spread [in centuries] between the people of this generation, and the scene of His crucifixion, yet He still lives.

Herod could not destroy Him, and the grave could not hold Him.

He stands forth upon the highest pinnacle of Heavenly glory, proclaimed of God, acknowledged by angels, adored by saints, and feared by devils, as the living, personal Christ, our Lord, our Savior, and our God.[2]

"Jesus, why did you come?"

Listen to Christ as He says, "I came as the Son of the Living God to offer myself as a Perfect Sacrifice,

---

[2] Republished as "The Incomparable Christ".

to honor the Covenant of Redemption, first stated in the Garden of Eden."

"Lord, is that the only reason why you came?"

"No, I also came to destroy the works of the Devil" (1 John 3:8).

Lying is a work of the Devil, as Satan lied in the Garden of Eden. "Now the serpent was more subtle than any beast of the field which the Lord God had made. And he said unto the woman, 'Yea, hath God said, "Ye shall not eat of every tree of the garden?"' And the woman said unto the serpent, 'We may eat of the fruit of the trees of the garden: but of the fruit of the tree which is in the midst of the garden, God hath said, "Ye shall not eat of it, neither shall ye touch it, lest ye die."' And the serpent said unto the woman, 'Ye shall not surely die: for God doth know that in the day ye eat thereof, then your eyes shall be opened, and ye shall be as gods, knowing good and evil'" (Genesis 3:1–5).

St. Augustine reminds us that, "When regard for truth has been broken down, or even slightly weakened, all things will remain doubtful."

A.W. Tozer warned, "The unattended garden will soon be overrun with weeds; the heart that fails to cultivate truth, and root out error, will shortly be a theological wilderness."

Murder is a work of the Devil. We read of how Cain, motivated by Satan rose up and murdered his righteous brother Abel. "In this the children of God, are manifest, and the Children of the devil: whosoever doth not righteousness is not of God, neither he that loveth not his brother. For this is the message that ye heard from the beginning, that we should love one another. Not as Cain, who was of that wicked one, and slew his brother. And wherefore slew he him? Because his own works were evil, and his brother's righteous" (1 John 3:10–12).

Moving men to pride is a work of the Devil, manifested in the Divine narrative of how the Evil One moved David to number the children of Israel. "And Satan stood up against Israel, and provoked David to number Israel . . . And God was displeased with this thing; therefore he smote Israel. . . . And the Lord spake unto Gad, David's seer, saying, 'Go and tell David, saying, "Thus saith the Lord, I offer thee three things: choose thee One of them, that I may do it unto thee." . . . And David said Unto Gad, 'I am in a great strait: let me fall now into the Hand of the Lord; for very great are His mercies: but let Me not fall into the hand of man'" (1 Chronicles 21:1, 7, 9–14).

The nation of Israel paid a terrible price for the pride of one man. Someone has said that we are never more like Satan himself than when we are filled with pride. Pride can make individuals unwilling to repent, unwilling to say, "I'm sorry," unwilling to tell the truth about things that all the world knows to be different. The Bible declares that God will always resist the proud, but He will give grace to the humble.

Betrayal is a work of the Devil, reflected in the fact that for 30 pieces of silver Judas betrayed the Son of God after the Devil had entered into him. "Now there was leaning on Jesus' bosom one of his Disciples, whom Jesus loved. Simon Peter therefore beckoned to him, that he should ask who it should be of whom he spake. He then lying on Jesus' breast saith unto him, 'Lord, who is it?' Jesus answered, 'He it is, to whom I shall give a sop, when I have dipped it.' And when he had dipped the sop, he gave it to Judas Iscariot, the son of Simon. And after the sop Satan entered into him. Then said Jesus unto him, 'That thou doest, do quickly'" (John 13:23–30).

There are many forms of betrayal such as a contract not honored, or re-negotiated, a friendship abused for selfish purposes, and a willingness to advance one's own agenda at all cost. The story is told of William Tyndale and how he was betrayed. Tyndale was the first person to translate the Bible from Hebrew and Greek into English. He wanted to make a Bible for the common people. He thought that a plowboy of ten with a Bible could know more than the Pope himself without the Scriptures. But the church officials stepped in to forbid Tyndale from giving the Bible to common people. Tyndale continued his work in secret, until, in 1535, a friend betrayed him. He was taken prisoner to the English castle of Vilford, where he still tried to continue his work. He was unable to finish his translation because he was sentenced to die a heretic's death. This involved strangulation and burning at the stake. On October 6, 1536, he spoke his last words, "Lord, open the eyes of the king of England." William Tyndale was a victim of betrayal and treachery.

Now Christ has come to destroy all the works of the Devil. And where Christ puts forth His strength, He overthrows the Evil One, as well as sin. John teaches those who are born of God are not in bondage to sin (1 John 3:9).

This, however, does not mean believers are endowed with angelic purity, though the Pelagians and the Cathari taught that during the days of John Calvin in the 16th century. Nor does it mean that believers are entirely sanctified, so that they are without sin, as some of the followers of John Wesley teach.

What it does mean, by contrast, is that "in the end of regeneration, sin will be destroyed and all who are begotten of God will live righteously and godly because God's Spirit corrects the lusting of sin" (John Calvin).

"Jesus, why did you come?"

"I came to destroy the works of the Devil."

"Lord, is that all?"

"No, I also came to seek and to save that which is lost, and to give eternal life to all who will believe." Because eternal life is a relationship with the Living Lord, based upon faith in all that Jesus claimed to be, the content of belief is important.

George Whitefield was preaching to coal miners in England. He asked one man, "What do you believe?"

"Well, I believe the same as the church."

"And what does the church believe?"

"Well, they believe the same as me."

Seeing he was getting nowhere, Whitefield said, "And what is it that you both believe?"

"Well, I suppose the same thing."

The coal miner lacked real content for faith. The content of faith is the gospel (1 Corinthians 1—3). The object of saving faith is Christ. But faith in Christ must not be in the abstract. It must be personal and real.

"The life of Christianity consists of possessive pronouns," says Martin Luther.

It is one thing to say, "Christ is a Savior". It is quite another thing to say, "He is my Savior and my Lord." The devil can say the first, but only the true Christian alone can say the second.

"Jesus, why did you come?"

"I came to honor the Covenant of Redemption. I came to destroy the works of the Devil. I came to seek and to save the lost. I came to give eternal life. I came so that individuals might say, 'Jesus is my Lord and my Savior.' Amen."

2

A Day of Triumph

The Bible gives a large amount of attention to the Triumphal Entry of Christ into the City of Jerusalem on the day which is called Palm Sunday.

"And when he had thus spoken, he went before, ascending up to Jerusalem. And it came to pass, when he was come nigh to Bethphage and Bethany, at the mount called the mount of Olives, he sent two of his disciples, saying, 'Go ye into the village over against you; in the which at your entering ye shall find a colt tied, whereon yet never man sat: loose him, and bring him hither. And if any man ask you, "Why do ye loose him?" Thus shall ye say unto him, "because the Lord hath need of him"'" (Luke 19:28–31).

There is a little more information given in Matthew's Gospel of this event, for Matthew's Gospel was written for a Jewish audience. Matthew notes, "All this was done, that it might be fulfilled which was spoken by the prophet, saying, 'Tell ye the daughter of Zion, Behold, thy King cometh unto thee, meek, and sitting upon an ass, and a colt the foal of an ass'" (Matthew 21:4–6).

There are more allusions, or references, to the Old Testament in Matthew's Gospel than in the other Gospels. The desire of Matthew was to remind his Jewish readers of the connection between the Old Testament Messiah and the New Testament person and work of Jesus.

In the Triumphal Entry, Jesus fully disclosed something He had been careful to keep relatively hidden to this point, and that was, He was the fulfillment of all the Old Testament prophecies concerning the Messiah. For this reason, Jesus came riding on a donkey, and not on a white charger or in a golden chariot. Scripture must be fulfilled.

"And the disciples went, and did as Jesus commanded them, and brought the ass, and the colt, and put on them their clothes, and they set him thereon. And a very great multitude spread their garments in the way; others cut down branches from the trees, and strewed them in the way. And the multitudes that went before, and that followed, cried, saying, 'Hosanna to the Son of David: Blessed is he that cometh in the name of the Lord; Hosanna in the highest.' And when he was come into Jerusalem, all the city was moved, saying, 'Who is this?' And the multitude said, 'This is Jesus the prophet of Nazareth of Galilee'" (Matthew 21:6–11).

When the people cried out, "Hosanna in the highest," they were honoring Jesus as a dignitary, much like people today might say about a special occasion, "We will roll out a red carpet." Jesus' Red-Carpet moment was significant as people made a comfortable place for Him to sit as they placed clothing on the back of the donkey. The donkey was a small animal in Israel. Then the people threw their clothing in the pathway the donkey was to travel as a gesture of honor and celebration.

There is a lovely story that Sir Walter Raleigh once laid his cloak over a mud puddle to keep Queen Elizabeth I from getting her feet wet. On another occasion, Raleigh caught the queen's attention in 1581 when he urged England to conquer Ireland. The queen rewarded him with extensive landholdings in

England and Ireland, knighted him in 1584, and named him captain of the queen's guard two years later.

However, an illicit affair with one of the queen's maids of honor in 1592 caused trouble. Sir Walter was imprisoned in the Tower of London, and ultimately, beheaded for treachery.

The story of the cloak and the mud puddle probably originated with historian Thomas Fuller who was known for embellishing facts.[3]

When the people placed their clothing at the feet of Jesus, they were treating Him as the coming King. This was reserved for royalty. They also placed palm branches before the Lord. Many were waving their arms at Jesus as they lined up along the street. And they were shouting, "Hosanna to the Son of David: Blessed is he that cometh in the name of the Lord; Hosanna in the highest." It was a spectacular moment.

The word "Hosanna," is a term of exaltation and adoration. Hosanna was also an ancient term used in association with palm branches. The idea was that a palm branch was used to signify a great victory. As a means of celebrating a great victory, the people

---

[3] See *10 Historical Misconceptions*, Publications International, Ltd.

would wave a hosanna, a palm branch, accompanied by a shout of acclamation, or a shout of victory. The palm branch signified victory.

Why is that important? Because Jesus was going to the Cross. But He was not going to a defeat, but to His victory over sin, Satan, and death itself. Without realizing it, the people in the crowd on that Palm Sunday were celebrating the victory the King of kings would win.

It is often observed that the same crowd became fickle just a few days later, to cry out against Jesus, shouting, "Crucify Him!" "Crucify Him!" It is said that this was done because the expectations of the people concerning Christ were not realized. Perhaps that is true. Still, for one brief shining moment there was the shout of victory, to the point, that the Pharisees circulating in the crowd wanted Jesus to silence His disciples.

"And when he was come nigh, even now at the descent of the mount of Olives, the whole multitude of the disciples began to rejoice and praise God with a loud voice for all the mighty works that they had seen; saying, 'Blessed be the King that cometh in the name of the Lord: peace in heaven, and glory in the highest.' And some of the Pharisees from among the multitude said unto him, 'Master, rebuke thy disciples'" (Luke 19:37–39).

The religious establishment was upset with Jesus. They regarded His ministry as a threat to the teaching and the Jewish heritage. So they rebuked Jesus, and told Him in turn to rebuke His disciples. "Just tell them to hush!"

But Jesus would not do that. "And he answered and said unto them, 'I tell you that, if these should hold their peace, the stones would immediately cry out'" (Luke 19:40). Jesus refused to rebuke His disciples on Palm Sunday, because there was a cosmic significance to this moment. Jesus was not simply the leader of a small radical religious group. His central message has been that the Kingdom of God was in the midst of the people, and He is the King of that Kingdom, of which there shall be no end. Jesus was God's appointed King who was entering into Jerusalem. Jesus was not some fleshly king of human origin. He is the King of kings to whom all knees shall bow. He is a cosmic King. His rule extends not only over all the earth, but over the whole universe. Therefore shout! Shout for the King's victory! People must not be blind and dumb by refusing to recognize the manifestation of God in their midst.

Historically, through the prophets, the LORD lamented, that, "The ox knoweth his owner, and the ass his master's crib: but Israel doth not know, my people doth not consider" (Isaiah 1:3). That changed on Palm Sunday. The disciples of Christ know the Scriptures. And they know their Messiah. If the disciples of Christ were rebuked, then the cosmos, the rocks, the universe itself must break out in praise to the King. So the stones had more sense than the Pharisees.

Beginning from the Mount of Olives, Jesus wound his way down the slope, around the Kedron Valley, and into the entrance of the City of Jerusalem, allowing the crowd to grow larger and larger still. He was received as a King, a Conquering King, a Victorious King. Church, "Behold your King!"

The concept of the Messiah as coming King was rooted in Jewish tradition, and so was the idea of the King giving a hosanna to His followers.

"I Esdras saw upon the mount Zion a great people, whom I could not number, and they all praised the Lord with songs. And in the midst of them there was a young man of a high stature, taller than all the rest, and upon every one of their heads he set crowns, and was more exalted; which I marvelled at greatly. So I asked the angel, and said, 'Sir, what are these?' He answered and said unto me, 'These are they that have put off the mortal clothing, and put on the immortal, and have confessed the name of God: now are they crowned, and receive palms.' Then said I unto the angel, 'What young person is it that crowneth them, and giveth them palms in their hands?' So he answered and said unto me, 'It is the Son of God, whom they have confessed in the world.' Then began I greatly to commend them that stood so stiffly for the name of the Lord. Then the angel said unto me, 'Go thy way, and tell my people what manner of things, and how great wonders of the Lord thy God, thou hast seen'" (2 Esdras 2:42–48).

Let the people of God rejoice. The King has come and will reward all who celebrate His victory. Come then, to the King of the kingdom. Bow before Him. Enter into His victory over sin, death, and destruction.

3

The Doctrine Jesus Taught

The Christian is to be committed to Christ and to the teachings of the Master. In John 5:17–47 Jesus taught about a variety of issues that must be understood and embraced.

Jesus taught the doctrine of the trinity. By declaring that He must engage in the great work of redemption, Christ taught His own equality with the Father. Even if many today do not understand, Jesus was claiming divinity for Himself. The Jews of His day did understand, for they took up stones to kill Him. John 5:17, "But Jesus answered them, 'My Father worketh hitherto, and I work.' Therefore the Jews sought the more to kill him, because he not only had broken the Sabbath, but said also that God was his Father, making himself equal with God."

Jesus taught the love of the Father for the Son. John 5:20, "For the Father loveth the Son, and sheweth him all things that himself doeth: and he will shew him greater works than these, [for the very purpose] that ye may marvel."

Jesus taught the physical resurrection of the dead. John 5:21, "For as the Father raiseth up the dead, and quickeneth them; even so the Son quickeneth whom he will."

Jesus taught the doctrine of selective spiritual election resulting in regeneration. John 5:21, "For as the Father raiseth up the dead, and quickeneth them; even so the Son quickeneth whom he will."

Jesus taught the doctrine of the judgment. John 5:22, "For the Father judgeth no man, but hath committed all judgment unto the Son: [in order] that all men should honor the Son, even as they honor the Father. He that honoureth not the Son honoureth not the Father which hath sent him. . . . For as the Father hath life in himself; so hath he given to the Son to have life in himself; and hath given him authority to execute judgment also, because he is the Son of man."

Jesus taught the doctrine of salvation by grace, through faith alone. John 5:24, "Verily, verily, I say unto you, He that heareth my word, and believeth on him that sent me, hath everlasting life, and shall not come into condemnation; but is passed from death unto life."

Jesus taught the doctrine of everlasting life. John 5:24, "Verily, verily, I say unto you, He that heareth my word, and believeth on him that sent me, hath everlasting life, and shall not come into condemnation; but is passed from death unto life."

Jesus taught the first resurrection is a spiritual resurrection. John 5:25, "Verily, verily, I say unto you, The hour is coming, and now is, when the dead shall hear the voice of the Son of God: and they that hear shall live." Revelation 20:6, "Blessed and holy is he that hath part in the first resurrection: on such the second death hath no power, but they shall be priests of God and of Christ, and shall reign with him a thousand years."

Jesus taught a singular general resurrection of the dead. John 5:28, "Marvel not at this: for the hour is coming, in the which all that are in the graves shall hear his voice, And shall come forth; they that have done good, unto the resurrection of life; and they that have done evil, unto the resurrection of damnation."

Jesus taught His own subordination to the Father. John 5:30, "I can of mine own self do nothing: as I hear, I judge: and my judgment is just; because I seek not mine own will, but the will of the Father which hath sent me. If I bear witness of myself, my witness is not true."

Jesus taught He was approved of God, and superior to John. John 5:32, "There is another that beareth witness of me; and I know that the witness which he witnesseth of me is true. Ye sent unto John, and he bare witness unto the truth. But I receive not testimony from man: but these things I say, that ye might be saved. He was a burning and a shining light: and ye were willing for a season to rejoice in his light. But I have greater witness than that of John: for the works which the Father hath given me to finish, the same works that I do, bear witness of me, that the Father hath sent me."

Jesus taught the Father is inscrutable. John 5:37, "And the Father himself, which hath sent me, hath borne witness of me. Ye have neither heard his voice at any time, nor seen his shape."

Jesus taught that not all people have the Word of God abiding in their hearts, nor will all men come to Him for salvation. The doctrine of universalism is in error. John 5:38–40, "And ye have not his word abiding in you: for whom he hath sent, him ye believe not. Search the scriptures; for in them ye think ye have eternal life: and they are they which testify of me. And ye will not come to me, that ye might have life."

Jesus taught it is possible to know if people do not have the love of God in their hearts. John 5:42, "But I know you, that ye have not the love of God in you."

Jesus taught that the Old Testament Scriptures spoke of Him. John 5:45, "Do not think that I will accuse you to the Father: there is one that accuseth you, even Moses, in whom ye trust. For had ye believed Moses, ye would have believed me: for he wrote of me. But if ye believe not his writings, how shall ye believe my words?"

4

Jesus and His Transfiguration

The story of the transfiguration of Jesus is recorded in Matthew 17.

"And after six days Jesus taketh Peter, James, and John his brother, and bringeth them up into a high mountain apart, and was transfigured before them: and his face did shine as the sun, and his raiment was white as the light. And, behold, there appeared unto them Moses and Elias talking with him. Then answered Peter, and said unto Jesus, 'Lord, it is good for us to be here: if thou wilt, let us make here three tabernacles; one for thee, and one for Moses, and one for Elias.' While he yet spake, behold, a bright cloud overshadowed them: and behold a voice out of the cloud, which said, 'This is my beloved Son, in whom

I am well pleased; hear ye him.' And when the disciples heard it, they fell on their face, and were sore afraid. And Jesus came and touched them, and said, 'Arise, and be not afraid.' And when they had lifted up their eyes, they saw no man, save Jesus only. And as they came down from the mountain, Jesus charged them, saying, 'Tell the vision to no man, until the Son of man be risen again from the dead'" (Matthew 17:1–9).

In the transfiguration of Christ, His majestic glory was manifested as it burst forth through the shield of His human nature which, for the most part, concealed His deity during the days of His humiliation. The three disciples, Peter, James, and John, who witnessed the transfiguration were never the same. They were eye witnesses of His glory.

John wrote that, "And the Word was made flesh, and dwelt among us, (and we beheld his glory, the glory as of the only begotten of the Father,) full of grace and truth" (John 1:14).

Peter said of Jesus, that He, "received from God the Father honor and glory, when there came such a voice to him from the excellent glory, 'This is my beloved Son, in whom I am well pleased.' And this voice which came from heaven we heard, when we were with him in the holy mount" (2 Peter 1:17–18).

The idea of glory is a theme that is central to the Bible. It is the focal point of all worship of God, reflected in part by the singing of the Doxology, from the Greek word for glory [*doxa* (dox´ah)]. The Hebrew word for glory [*kabowed* (kaw-bode)] refers to a weight. Figuratively, in a good sense, the glory of God is "weighty" because it is full of splendor and honor. The weightiness of God is found in His exalted dignity and majesty. When the Church sings the doxology, it is because the hearts of the people of God are trying to gather in the glory of God.

> Praise God, from whom all blessings flow;
> Praise Him, all creatures here below;
> Praise Him above, ye heav'nly host;
> Praise Father, Son, and Holy Ghost.
> *Amen.*

When the Church sings the *Gloria Patri*, the message is rooted in an affirmation of the Trinity, despite the controversy that surrounds that deep doctrine. Glory is attributed to God the Father, God the Son, and God the Holy Spirit, because glory is an attribute of the Divine.

Glory be to the Father
and to the Son and to the Holy Ghost,
as it was in the beginning
is now, and ever shall be,
world without end.
Amen, amen.

In the life of Jesus there is revealed a glimpse of Divine glory when the second member of the Trinity was transfigured during the days of His humanity. Though Jesus became a man, God has highly exalted Him. "Let this mind be in you, which was also in Christ Jesus: Who, being in the form of God, thought it not robbery to be equal with God: but made himself of no reputation, and took upon him the form of a servant, and was made in the likeness of men: and being found in fashion as a man, he humbled himself, and became obedient unto death, even the death of the cross. Wherefore God also hath highly exalted him, and given him a name which is above every name: that at the name of Jesus every knee should bow, of things in heaven, and things in earth, and things under the earth; and that every tongue should confess that Jesus Christ is Lord, to the glory of God the Father" (Philippians 2:5–11).

The question comes: "What did Jesus empty Himself of?" In Liberal Theology, in the Death of God community of the 19th century and following, speculative theologians said that what Jesus emptied Himself of was His deity, called *kenosis*.

In response, conservative theologian Benjamin B. Warfield said that the only *kenosis* that theory proved, was the *kenosis* (emptiness) of the brains of those who espoused it. God cannot stop being God. What Jesus did lay aside was the glory of His divine prerogative, and allowed Himself to be treated beneath His dignity. He allowed Himself to be treated as a slave, even though He is LORD of all. But even His glory was not completely laid aside as Matthew 17 reveals.

In the Old Testament economy, the most common expression of the glory of God was the *Shekinah*, or that cloud that spoke of God's residence or dwelling (i.e., His *Shekinah*). This term is not used in Scripture, but was later used by Jews and Christian writers, based on Scriptural passages. "And the Lord went before them by day in a pillar of a cloud, to lead them the way; and by night in a pillar of fire, to give them light; to go by day and night: He took not away the pillar of the cloud by day, nor the pillar of fire by night, from before the people" (Exodus 13:21). "And he said, I beseech You, show me Your glory" (Exodus 33:18).

When Jesus returns to earth, He will return in dazzling light, for He shall come on clouds of glory. The *Shekinah* shall blaze the way for Him. "And Jesus said, I am: and ye shall see the Son of man sitting on the right hand of power, and coming in the clouds of heaven" (Mark 14:62).

In anticipation of the glory that shall come, Peter, James, and John, were witnesses of the glory of Christ in His transfiguration. This event occurred six days after the Philippi of Caesarea confession by Peter, whereby Simon Peter said to Jesus, "Thou art the Christ, the Son of the living God" (Matthew 16:16).

Taking this inner circle to a high mountain, Jesus was transfigured, or experienced a metamorphous in their presence. Morphology is the study of form or structure. The form or structure of Christ was changed. Something dramatic took place so that the face of Jesus "did shine as the sun, and his raiment was white as the light" (Matthew 17:2).

When Mark gives his account, he adds a detail by saying that the raiment of Christ "became shining," and whiter than what a professional launder could do (Mark 9:3). This visible description of the clothing of Christ spoke of whiteness that no earthly fuller could improve upon. The lesson is that the righteousness of Christ and His purity is so complete that it cannot be improved upon. Such a description could never be applicable to a mere human. Therefore, the divinity of Christ was on display in the transfiguration.

Moses once prayed, "I beseech You, show me Your Glory" (Exodus 33:18). The glory of God was revealed to Moses, and then, in Christ, the glory of God was revealed again. But there is an important difference. When Moses saw the glory of God, he saw only a reflected glory which caused his face to glow afterwards. "And he said, Thou canst not see my face: for there shall no man see me, and live. And the Lord said, 'Behold, there is a place by me, and thou shalt stand upon a rock: and it shall come to pass, while my glory passeth by, that I will put thee in a clift of the rock, and will cover thee with my hand while I pass by'" (Exodus 33:20–22). "And the children of Israel saw the face of Moses, that the skin of Moses' face shone: and Moses put the veil upon his face again, until he went in to speak with him" (Exodus 34:35).

The glory that Moses enjoyed was a reflected glory, while the glory that surrounded Christ was intrinsic to Himself. The light shown forth from the face of Christ, and it was not reflected onto Him in any external way. In Christ, the inherent, internal light of the glory of God was bursting out of Christ's being. He himself is the source of the light. He himself is the source of the whiteness that His divinity was bursting forth from the cloak of His humanity. While this moment was taking place, something else extraordinary happened. Moses and Elijah appeared to represent the Law and the Prophets. A conversation took place about the impending death of Christ.

Suddenly, Peter spoke up. Speaking to Jesus, Peter said, "Lord, it is good for us to be here: if thou wilt, let us make here three tabernacles; one for thee, and one for Moses, and one for Elias" (Matthew 17:4). "While he yet spake, behold, a bright cloud overshadowed them: and behold a voice out of the cloud, which said, 'This is my beloved Son, in whom I am well pleased; hear ye him.' And when the disciples heard it, they fell on their face, and were sore afraid" (Matthew 17:5–6).

When the disciples saw the unveiled glory of Christ, when the disciples saw the Shekinah glory, they were afraid. The disciples were terrified and fell on their faces before Him. Why? Hebrews 1 explains. The disciples saw the One who is the brightness of the Father's glory. "God, who at sundry times and in divers manners spake in time past unto the fathers by the prophets, hath in these last days spoken unto us by his Son, whom he hath appointed heir of all things, by whom also he made the worlds; who being the brightness of his glory, and the express image of his person, and upholding all things by the word of his power, when he had by himself purged our sins, sat down on the right hand of the Majesty on high" (Hebrews 1:1–3).

So great the glory of God and the brightness of the Son, there is no need for a physical sun to illuminate the heavenly city. The radiance of the glory of God will never be diminished. "And there shall be no night there; and they need no candle, neither light of the sun; for the Lord God giveth them light: and they shall reign for ever and ever" (Revelation 22:5).

Seeing the disciples on their faces in fear, Jesus went and touched them. The glory had passed. Moses was gone. Elijah was gone. But, the memory remained. After the resurrection, the disciples remembered the glory they had seen, and told the world.

5

I AM *the Bread of Life*

"And Jesus said unto them, I am the bread of life: he that cometh to me shall never hunger; and he that believeth on me shall never thirst" (John 6:35).

Different individuals have stated who they think Jesus is.

Demons. "And devils also came out of many, crying out, and saying, 'Thou art Christ the Son of God.' And he rebuking them suffered them not to speak: for they knew that he was Christ" (Luke 4:41).

Pharisees. "The disciple is not above his master, nor the servant above his lord. It is enough for the disciple that he be as his master, and the servant as his lord. If they have called the master of the house

Beelzebub, how much more shall they call them of his household?" (Matthew 10:24–25).

Nicodemus. "There was a man of the Pharisees, named Nicodemus, a ruler of the Jews: The same came to Jesus by night, and said unto him, 'Rabbi, we know that thou art a teacher come from God: for no man can do these miracles that thou doest, except God be with him'" (John 3:1–2).

Men. "When Jesus came into the coasts of Caesarea Philippi, he asked his disciples, saying, 'Whom do men say that I the Son of man am?' And they said, 'Some say that thou art John the Baptist: some, Elias; and others, Jeremias, or one of the prophets'" (Matthew 16:13).

Peter. "He saith unto them, 'But whom say ye that I am?' And Simon Peter answered and said, 'Thou art the Christ, the Son of the living God'" (Matthew 16:15–16).

More importantly is what Jesus called Himself.

Jesus is the Bread of Life. John 6:35, "And Jesus said unto them, 'I am the bread of life: he that cometh to me shall never hunger; and he that believeth on me shall never thirst.'"

Jesus is the Light of the World. "Then spake Jesus again unto them, saying, 'I am the light of the world:

he that followeth me shall not walk in darkness, but shall have the light of life'" (John 8:12).

Jesus is the Door. "Then said Jesus unto them again, 'Verily, verily, I say unto you, I am the door of the sheep'" (John 10:7).

Jesus is the Good Shepherd. "I am the good shepherd: the good shepherd giveth his life for the sheep" (John 10:11).

Jesus is the Resurrection. "Jesus said unto her, 'I am the resurrection, and the life: he that believeth in me, though he were dead, yet shall he live'" (John 11:25).

Jesus is the Way. "Jesus saith unto him, 'I am the way, the truth, and the life: no man cometh unto the Father, but by me'" (John 14:6).

Jesus is the Vine. "I am the true vine, and my Father is the husbandman" (John 15:1).

Each statement of Jesus reveals something of His own understanding.

The context for the Bread of Life Discourse was the desire of the Jews to be given a sign by Jesus that He was authentic, that He was sent by God, and that a reason would be provided as to why individuals should believe in Him. "They said therefore unto him, 'What sign showest thou then, that we may see, and believe thee? What dost thou work?'" (John 6:30).

The Jews based their demand for a sign from Jesus on the historical fact that God gave to all the people of Israel a sign, in the form of manna from heaven. Picking up on their historical appeal, Jesus interpreted the true meaning of that sign and identified Himself with it. "Then Jesus said unto them, 'Verily, verily, I say unto you, Moses gave you not that bread from heaven; but my Father giveth you the true bread from heaven. For the bread of God is he which cometh down from heaven, and giveth life unto the world'" (John 6:32–33).

Normally, in the Greek, when a person wanted to say, "I am", they would say, "*ego*", which is where the English word originates. But the Greek language has another word, "*eimi*" which can be translated, "I am." What is unique with Jesus is that He says, "*Ego emi*", or, "I am the bread of life."

This form of speaking, "*ego emi*", is very rare, but it can be found in the Septuagint. When the Greek translators of the Old Testament came to Exodus 3:14, they translated the response of God to Moses, "I AM THAT I AM" with "*Ego eimi*." "And God said unto Moses, I AM THAT I AM: and he said, 'Thus shalt thou say unto the children of Israel, I AM hath sent me unto you'" (Ex. 3:14).

In the New Testament, Jesus took that unusual reference for Himself thereby making Himself equal to God. In other words, the divine name God gave to Moses (I AM), Jesus ascribed to Himself. He actually, truly, verily called Himself God (I AM). Technically speaking, if we were to offer a direct translation of the Greek into English, the words of Jesus would be given this way: "The bread of life, I AM." The response of Jesus is significant as the Lord made some critical points. It was the Father, not Moses, who gave the manna from heaven. The true manna from heaven, the most significant manna from heaven, is not physical bread, but Himself, the Son of God, who can give eternal life to all who believe. Jesus saw Himself as coming, not from Judah, not from Bethlehem, but from heaven. John 3:13 says, "And no man hath ascended up to heaven, but he that came down from heaven, even the Son of man which is in heaven."

Later, the church would declare the ascension of Christ, and thus, His exaltation in heaven at the right hand of the Father. Jesus simply returned to the place from which He came. The response of the Jews is recorded. "Then said they unto him, 'Lord, evermore give us this bread'" (John 6:34).

When truth is spoken and illuminated by God the Holy Spirit to a darkened heart, there is a positive reaction to the gospel. It is an exhilarating moment. The heart cries out for more. The heard cries out, "Lord, give us this bread."

As the Bread of Life Discourse continued, Jesus taught the Doctrine of Man's Inability to come to Christ on his own, and the Doctrine of Divine Election. Simply stated, the Doctrine of Election teaches that, from the sea of humanity, before the foundation of the world, the Father gave certain individuals to Christ to become the heirs of His redemptive work and thus salvation. All that the Father has given to the Son will come to Him. There is a divine certainty. "And Jesus said unto them, 'I am the bread of life: he that cometh to me shall never hunger; and he that believeth on me shall never thirst. But I said unto you, That ye also have seen me, and believe not. All that the Father giveth me shall come to me; and him that cometh to me I will in no wise cast out. For I came down from heaven, not to do mine own will, but the will of him that sent me. And this is the Father's will which hath sent me, that of all which he hath given me I should lose nothing, but should raise it up again at the last day. And this is the will of him that sent me, that everyone which seeth the Son, and believeth on him, may have everlasting life: and I will raise him up at the last day'" (John 6:35).

Baptist history has traditionally embraced the Biblical teaching concerning man's total inability to save himself and the need for God's effectual and electing love to be manifested towards him.

The Baptist Confession of Faith, 1689
Chapter 3: Of God's Decree. Paragraph 7.

"The doctrine of the high mystery of predestination is to be handled with special prudence and care, that men attending the will of God revealed in His Word, and yielding obedience thereunto, may, from the certainty of their effectual vocation, be assured of their eternal election; so shall this doctrine afford matter of praise, reverence, and admiration of God, and of humility, diligence, and abundant consolation to all that sincerely obey the gospel."

The Baptist Faith and Message, June 14, 2000
Article 5: God's Purpose of Grace

"Election is the gracious purpose of God, according to which He regenerates, justifies, sanctifies, and glorifies sinners. It is consistent with the free agency of man, and comprehends all the means in connection with the end. It is the glorious display of God's sovereign goodness, and is infinitely wise, holy, and unchangeable. It excludes boasting and promotes humility."

* * *

Picking up on the idea that Jesus said He came from heaven, the Jews began to murmur at Him, for they knew the Lord's father, Joseph, and his mother, Mary. "The Jews then murmured at him, because he said, 'I am the bread which came down from heaven.' And they said, 'Is not this Jesus, the son of Joseph, whose father and mother we know? How is it then that he saith, "I came down from heaven?"'" (John 6:41).

Jesus immediately moved to silence the murmuring of the Jews by teaching the Doctrine of

Election. There is a body of people whom the Father has given to the Son. These people will be drawn to Christ; they will be dragged to Christ and will be raised up at the last day. "Jesus therefore answered and said unto them, 'Murmur not among yourselves. No man can come to me, except the Father which hath sent me draw him: and I will raise him up at the last day'" (John 6:43). The prophet wrote, "He shall see of the travail of his soul, and shall be satisfied: by his knowledge shall my righteous servant justify many; for he shall bear their iniquities" (Isaiah 53:11).

Jesus spoke of man's natural inability to come to Christ. "No man can come to me, except the Father which hath sent me draw him: and I will raise him up at the last day" (John 6:44). The word "except," means "unless," and refers to a necessary condition which must occur in order for something to take place. What must occur prior to a person coming to Christ is the drawing of the Father. As the leopard cannot change the spots on the skin, the natural man cannot come to Christ except the Father draws him.

The word for draw (*helkuo*, hel-koo'-o), to drag (literally or figuratively) means, "to compel." The Father does not "woo" the sinner, or try to entice him. The drawing of the Father is effective. When a person is drawn by the Father to Jesus, the person does come to Christ, for the inner disposition of the person is changed by the Holy Spirit. Regeneration precedes salvation, so that upon gospel hearing, the Bread of Life is desired.

"It is written in the prophets, And they shall be all taught of God. Every man therefore that hath heard, and hath learned of the Father, cometh unto me. Not that any man hath seen the Father, save he which is of God, he hath seen the Father. Verily, verily, I say unto you, He that believeth on me hath everlasting life. I am that bread of life. Your fathers did eat manna in the wilderness, and are dead. This is the bread which cometh down from heaven, that a man may eat thereof, and not die. I am the living bread which came down from heaven: if any man eat of this bread, he shall live forever: and the bread that I will give is my flesh, which I will give for the life of the world" (John 6:45–51).

At the Last Supper, Jesus used similar language with His disciples. "And he took bread, and gave thanks, and brake it, and gave unto them, saying, 'This is my body which is given for you: this do in remembrance of me'" (Luke 22:19).

When the Lord taught the Doctrine of Man's Inability to save himself, and the Doctrine of Divine Election, the Jews resisted, and murmured against Him. Many abandoned Jesus. "From that time many of his disciples went back, and walked no more with him" (John 6:66). A true disciple will love the doctrine of Christ, and will eat of the Bread of Life, and shall live.

6

I AM *the Light of the World*

"Then spake Jesus again unto them, saying, 'I am the light of the world: he that followeth me shall not walk in darkness, but shall have the light of life'" (John 8:12).

The second "I AM" in Scripture is recorded in the Gospel of John. "Then spake Jesus again unto them, saying, 'I am the light of the world: he that followeth me shall not walk in darkness, but shall have the light of life'" (John 8:12). In some ancient manuscripts, this specific text does not occur here, but is placed in a different context. The statement of Christ is given following the story of the woman being dragged before Christ for condemnation. After she is dismissed, Jesus spoke to those who remained.

The term light is an important term in the Gospel of John. It is a metaphor for the truth of the gospel, the ministry of Christ, and what happens to people who are converted to the Lord. Light is a term that is contrasted with darkness. Individuals are described naturally as being children of darkness. "For ye were sometimes darkness, but now are ye light in the Lord: walk as children of light" (Ephesians 5:8).

Darkness refers to a moral deficiency leading to moral darkness. Joseph Conrad's novel, *The Heart of Darkness*, explores the depths of total depravity. The heart of darkness is a heart that lives in a state of corruption. There are works that are done in darkness. "And this is the condemnation, that light is come into the world, and men loved darkness rather than light, because their deeds were evil" (John 3:19).

Those who engage in works of virtue are not inclined to work in darkness. Isaiah spoke of a day that would come when people who walk in darkness would see a great light. "The people that walked in darkness have seen a great light: they that dwell in the land of the shadow of death, upon them hath the light shined" (Isaiah 9:2).

There is an antithesis in Scripture between light and darkness. Jesus is the light of the world that radiates the effulgent glory of God who is seen as being light. God is viewed as dwelling in light inaccessible. "Who only hath immortality, dwelling in the light which no man can approach unto; whom no man hath seen, nor can see: to whom be honor and power everlasting. Amen" (1 Timothy 6:16).

When God manifests Himself in Scripture, He does so with overpowering expressions of light. Jesus appeared in glory on the Mount of Transfiguration. "And after six days Jesus taketh Peter, James, and John his brother, and bringeth them up into an high mountain apart, And was transfigured before them: and his face did shine as the sun, and his raiment was white as the light" (Matthew 17:1).

Christ did not reflect light, but emanated it. The light of Christ came from within Him, and radiated outwardly, unlike Moses, whose face radiated the reflected glory he enjoyed by being with God. There was a reflected glory, not an inherent or intrinsic glory. "And the children of Israel saw the face of Moses that the skin of Moses' face shone: and Moses put the veil upon his face again, until he went in to speak with him" (Exodus 34:35).

Jesus appeared to Saul in a glory of light. "And as he journeyed, he came near Damascus: and suddenly there shined round about him a light from heaven" (Acts 9:3). The importance of light is seen in the fact that it gives color to objects. Without light, an orange, a shirt, or the universe has no color. It is the light that gives color to an item. Certain substances will refract certain colors of the light spectrum, while others are absorbed. Without the source of light, everything is black. There is no color.

In Christ there is color and glory, and His disciples were eyewitnesses to it. "And the Word was made flesh, and dwelt among us, (and we beheld his glory, the glory as of the only begotten of the Father,) full of grace and truth" (John 1:14).

Prior to John 8, Jesus had been spoken of by John as light. "In the beginning was the Word, and the Word was with God, and the Word was God. The same was in the beginning with God. All things were made by him; and without him was not anything made that was made. In him was life; and the life was the light of men. And the light shineth in darkness; and the darkness comprehended it not" (John 1:1–5).

The metaphor of light and darkness is not unique to Christian literature. It was a favorite metaphor of the Greek philosopher Plato. In his *The Republic*, Plato tells the story of slaves who are confined to the quarters in a cave. There is a little fire in the cave which reflects shadows on the walls in the cave. The slaves have no clear view of reality. Plato calls the shadows "opinion". He sees this as being less than true knowledge. In order to have true knowledge individuals have to get out of the cave, out of the shadows, out of the darkness, and into the noonday brightness of light. In the shining of the sun, the slaves can behold objects as they are. It is only in the context of light that reality be known in order to have knowledge.

In the second century, Justin Martyr argued that knowledge of God comes not only in the Bible, but through nature. "The heavens declare the glory of God; and the firmament sheweth his handywork" (Psalm 19:1).

Because of the light of nature many truths are revealed, even to the ungodly, that benefit humanity. Individuals can be philosophers, geologists, scientists, and mathematicians without believing in God, but ultimately, they operate within the limiting shadows of their unbelief. What John argued, what Christians today contend for, is that the Supreme Author of all knowledge and truth is Christ. In Christ the fullness of the godhead is bodily expressed. Christ is the one who imparts whatever light individuals have who come into the world.

Even when the Light is rejected, there are benefits that are enjoyed by the unbeliever. In the beginning, the universe was nothing but formlessness, emptiness, and darkness. Then God said, "Let there be light," and the angels sang in wonder and joy. The first act of God in creation was to bring light to a universe that was in darkness without it. "In the beginning God created the Heaven and the earth. And the earth was without form, and void; and darkness was upon the face of the deep. And the Spirit of God moved upon the face of the waters. And God said, 'Let there be light,' and there was light. And God saw the light, that it was good: and God divided the light from the darkness" (Genesis 1:1–4).

The end of biblical revelation contains the vivid relation of a new heaven and a new earth bathed, not in natural light, but with the light of the glory of God. "And there shall be no night there; and they need no candle, neither light of the sun; for the Lord God giveth them light: and they shall reign for ever and ever" (Revelation 22:5).

When a person becomes a Christian, new spiritual sight is given to see Christ in all of His splendor and glory. "Then spake Jesus again unto them, saying, 'I am the light of the world: he that followeth me shall not walk in darkness, but shall have the light of life.' The Pharisees therefore said unto him, 'Thou bearest record of thyself; thy record is not true.' Jesus answered and said unto them, 'Though I bear record of myself, yet my record is true: for I know whence I came, and whither I go; but ye cannot tell whence I come, and whither I go. Ye judge after the flesh; I judge no man. And yet if I judge, my judgment is true: for I am not alone, but I and the Father that sent me. It is also written in your law, that the testimony of two men is true. I am one that bear witness of myself, and the Father that sent me beareth witness of me.' Then said they unto him, 'Where is thy Father?' Jesus answered, 'Ye neither know me, nor my Father: if ye had known me, ye should have known my Father also'" (John 8:12–19).

When the Pharisees protested Jesus declaring Himself to be the Light of the world, the Lord declared, that legally, He had a witness, His Father. When God speaks there is no need for human collaboration. At the baptism of Jesus, the Father confirmed Jesus to be His Son, in whom He was pleased. "And lo a voice from heaven, saying, 'This is my beloved Son, in whom I am well pleased'" (Matthew 3:17).

Some of the Pharisees, such as Nicodemus, acknowledged the claims that Jesus did come from God. "There was a man of the Pharisees, named Nicodemus, a ruler of the Jews: The same came to Jesus by night, and said unto him, 'Rabbi, we know that thou art a teacher come from God: for no man can do these miracles that thou doest, except God be with him'" (John 3:1–2).

7

I AM *the* Door

"Then said Jesus unto them again, 'Verily, verily, I say unto you, I am the door of the sheep'" (John 10:7).

When Jesus used the formally, "I AM", He used the language that was reserved for God in the Septuagint, *ergo emi, ergo emi,* I AM. "And God said unto Moses, 'I AM THAT I AM,' and he said, 'Thus shalt thou say unto the children of Israel, I AM hath sent me unto you'" (Exodus 3:14).

The statement of Christ as being the Door is set against the backdrop of the healing of a blind man in John 9:1–34. It is also united to another "I AM," as Christ calls Himself the Good Shepherd.

I AM the Door. "Then said Jesus unto them again, 'Verily, verily, I say unto you, I am the door of the sheep'" (John 10:7).

I AM the Good Shepherd. "I am the good shepherd: the good shepherd giveth his life for the sheep" (John 10:11).

When Jesus called Himself the Door, or the entrance to the Sheep Gate, He was speaking to a generation who culturally understood the importance of keeping sheep. The Old Testament often mentions shepherds, and shepherding reflected in Psalm 23. The Jews were familiar with the keeping of sheep throughout Palestine. During the day the sheep were led to pastures, and then to still waters. At night, they were brought to a place that was protected and enclosed. It was called the sheepfold.

There were a variety of sheepfolds. Some were made out of wood. A fence was made to hedge the sheep. Often the sheepfold was made out of stones to form a very secure fortress. This would better protect the sheep from thieves or wild animals. A stone wall would also keep the sheep from being scattered if the wooden fence was destroyed in some manner. On top of the stone enclosure were briars with sharp needles to discourage the sheep from trying to jump over the wall, and to discourage predators from trying to get over the wall to steal or hurt the sheep.

Central to the sheepfold was the door. The door, or sheep gate, was the focus point to gaining access to the sheep in the fold. Through the door the sheep would enter to and exit from the fold. The shepherd would do the same. Often several herds were gathered into the sheepfold. Then, a gate keeper was appointed to guard the flock. The gate keeper was not necessarily a shepherd. He might simply be a hireling to guard the sheep.

When a shepherd did come to the sheepfold to gather his sheep, it was done easily enough by the shepherd calling to the sheep. The sheep recognized the voice of their shepherd and would follow him.

The first image Jesus used, in context, is to say, "I am the door." Initially, Jesus makes a distinction between the sheep gate keeper and the shepherd. The sheep gate keeper, or porter, will open the door to the shepherd. "To him the porter openeth; and the sheep hear his voice: and he calleth his own sheep by name, and leadeth them out" (John 10:3).

Once inside the sheepfold, the shepherd would stand in the middle of the herds and call his sheep, sometimes by name. The sheep would respond by gathering around their shepherd. They wanted to be with him. They followed him. "And when he putteth forth his own sheep, he goeth before them, and the sheep follow him: for they know his voice" (John 10:4).

The larger spiritual truth was conveying that God has a people. God has a flock of sheep. In the kingdom of heaven they are safely in the fold. They will be forever secure, for Jesus is the sheep-gate. He is the door to the sheepfold. He is the one who leads His own into a mighty fortress.

By saying that He was the door to the sheep fold, Jesus was not being politically correct or religiously sensitive. In modern polite society, Christians are rebuked for declaring there is One Way to heaven. But, they are correct. Jesus did not say that the sheepfold had ten different doors, and each of them was equally valid. There was only one door, Jesus Christ. "Neither is there salvation in any other: for there is none other name under heaven given among men, whereby we must be saved" (Acts 4:12). Nor did Jesus say that the sheepfold was inclusive. The sheepfold was for those who knew the voice of their shepherd. There is only one Shepherd.

The context for what Jesus was saying about the sheepfold was a healing miracle recorded in John 9. Following his healing, the man who was healed of his blindness was rejected by the religious leaders and cast out of the synagogue. "When Jesus heard the man had been cast out, he found him and said unto him, 'Dost thou believe on the Son of God?'" (John 9:35).

The man responded by asking, "Who is he, Lord that I might believe on him?" (John 9:36). It was at that moment Jesus revealed Himself, and the man believed and worshipped Jesus. "And Jesus said unto him, 'Thou hast both seen him, and it is he that talketh with thee.' And he said, 'Lord, I believe.' And he worshipped him" (John 9:37–38).

Some Pharisees, who were present for this transaction and heard the words of Jesus, were offended. They perceived that Jesus was directing comments to them. "For judgment I am come into this world, that they which see not might see; and that they which see might be made blind" (John 9:39).

With scathing sarcasm, the Pharisees asked, "Are we blind also?" (John 9:40). It was the wrong question to ask, for Christ immediately gave them an honest answer. Yes, they were blind. "Jesus said unto them, 'If ye were blind, ye should have no sin: but now ye say, "We see," therefore your sin remaineth'" (John 9:41).

The Pharisees were blind to the goodness of Jesus. A miracle had taken place in their midst, but they did not care. They were jealous that Jesus had performed the miracle and would get the glory, not them. They did not care that a member of their flock had been helped. The Pharisees were not only blind, they were ignorant. They did not know the benefits of going to Christ as the Door of the Sheep Gate.

Later, when the apostle Paul wrote his epistle to the Romans, he remembered the teaching of Jesus. Paul set forth two benefits of salvation. First, every soul has peace with God because of our justification. Second, every believer has access into God's grace. That is what a door does. It allows access. Paul taught what Jesus proclaimed about himself. "Therefore being justified by faith, we have peace with God through our Lord Jesus Christ; by whom also we have access by faith into this grace wherein we stand, and rejoice in hope of the glory of God" (Romans 5:1–2).

The normal means of access is through a door. Jesus is the Door through which people enter into heaven, and into the presence of God. This imagery is tied to the whole image of the barrier to the access. In the Garden of Eden, God posted a guard, to stop access to the Tree of Life. "So he drove out the man; and he placed at the east of the garden of Eden Cherubim and a flaming sword which turned every way, to keep the way of the tree of life" (Genesis 3:24).

In the Tabernacles, and later in the Temple, there was a barrier between God and men in the form of a curtain. Only the High Priest was allowed access into the Holy of Holies, and then, only one time a year. Sin is a barrier to God. The barrier of sin must be broken down before there is access to God. Christ provides that access. "For through him we both have access by one Spirit unto the Father" (Ephesians 2:18).

Christ is the access. Christ is the door into the Holy of Holies. In Christ, every believer can go through the curtain into the Holy of Holies. "Having therefore, brethren, boldness to enter into the holiest by the blood of Jesus, by a new and living way, which he hath consecrated for us, through the veil, that is to say, his flesh; and having an high priest over the house of God; let us draw near with a true heart in full assurance of faith, having our hearts sprinkled from an evil conscience, and our bodies washed with pure water" (Hebrews 10:19–22).

Do you believe this? Will you abandon, if necessary, society's pluralistic approach to religion? Are you willing to be controversial for Christ? Will you say, by faith, "Christ is the Door to salvation?" Will you affirm that, "Christ alone is the Sheep Gate." May God grant Christians holy boldness to teach others about the Great, I AM.

8

I AM *the Good Shepherd*

"I am the good shepherd: the good shepherd giveth his life for the sheep" (John 10:11).

In context, Jesus adds to His imagery of being the Door to the sheepfold. He is not only the Door, He is the Good Shepherd. The goodness of the Lord as Shepherd is reflected in the fact that He will give His life for the sheep.

In biblical terms, sheep speak of the elect of God. They have been chosen by the Father in eternity past and given to the Son. "My sheep hear my voice, and I know them, and they follow me, and I give unto them eternal life; and they shall never perish, neither shall any man pluck them out of my hand. My Father, which gave them me, is greater than all; and no man is able to pluck them out of my Father's hand" (John 10:27–29).

There are many things which the Father has given to the Son.

Great works to perform. "But I have greater witness than that of John: for the works which the Father hath given me to finish, the same works that I do, bear witness of me, that the Father hath sent me" (John 5:36).

A cup of wrath. "Then said Jesus unto Peter, 'Put up thy sword into the sheath: the cup which my Father hath given me, shall I not drink it?'" (John 18:11).

Sheep. "My sheep hear my voice, and I know them, and they follow me, and I give unto them eternal life; and they shall never perish, neither shall any man pluck them out of my hand. My Father, which gave them me, is greater than all; and no man is able to pluck them out of my Father's hand" (John 10:27).

All power. "And Jesus came and spake unto them, saying, 'All power is given unto me in heaven and in earth'" (Matthew 28:18).

All nations on earth. "Ask of me, and I shall give thee the heathen for thine inheritance, and the uttermost parts of the earth for thy possession" (Psalms 2:8).

The goodness of Christ as the Shepherd is contrasted with that of the hireling, who does not really care for the sheep. The hireling will leave the sheep to wolves, and will flee, because he does not own them. The Good Shepherd does own the sheep. "But he that is an hireling, and not the shepherd, whose own the sheep are not, seeth the wolf coming, and leaveth the sheep, and fleeth: and the wolf catcheth them, and scattereth the sheep. The hireling fleeth, because he is an hireling, and careth not for the sheep" (John 10:12–13).

Christ owns His sheep by right of redemption. He has purchased them with His own blood. "In whom we have redemption through his blood, the forgiveness of sins, according to the riches of his grace" (Ephesians 1:7).

In Psalm 23, David likens God to the Good Shepherd. The rod and staff God wielded comforted David. The rod was a defensive club. It was used to protect the sheep from wolves or thieves. The staff was an offense resource. It delivered the sheep from dangerous situations. The Lord's strength was there to protect David. "The Lord is my shepherd; I shall not want. He maketh me to lie down in green pastures: he leadeth me beside the still waters. He restoreth my soul: he leadeth me in the paths of righteousness for his name's sake. Yea, though I walk through the valley of the shadow of death, I will fear no evil: for thou art with me; thy rod and thy staff they comfort me" (Psalm 23:1–4).

David recalled his own days as a shepherd. He was willing to give his life for his sheep, too. When a bear came to devour the flock, David fought for the sheep. When a lion tried to carry a sheep off, David slew the lion. He was a good shepherd. "And David said unto Saul, 'Thy servant kept his father's sheep, and there came a lion, and a bear, and took a lamb out of the flock: And I went out after him, and smote him, and delivered it out of his mouth: and when he arose against me, I caught him by his beard, and smote him, and slew him'" (1 Samuel 17:34).

Later, David viewed all of Israel as the sheep of God. He was willing to fight a giant for them. He was worthy to be a Shepherd-King. "David said moreover, 'The Lord that delivered me out of the paw of the lion, and out of the paw of the bear, he will deliver me out of the hand of this Philistine.' And Saul said unto David, 'Go, and the Lord be with thee'" (1 Samuel 17:37). David was a type of Christ. He foreshadowed the Lord Jesus Christ as the Good Shepherd.

As the Good Shepherd, Jesus loves His sheep. He has their best interest in His heart. He defends His sheep unto death. When the Good Shepherd gives His life for His sheep, He makes it clear that no one is taking His life from Him. His sacrificial act is one of selflessness. "No man taketh it from me, but I lay it down of myself. I have power to lay it down, and I have power to take it again. This commandment have I received of my Father" (John 10:18).

Jesus knew He had legions of angels at His disposal to protect Him. "Thinkest thou that I cannot now pray to my Father, and he shall presently give me more than twelve legions of angels?" (Matthew 26:53).

> He could have called ten thousand angels,
> To destroy the world and set Him free.
> He could have called ten thousand angels,
> But He died alone for you and me.

Jesus told His captors they had not power over Him, except what was given them. "Jesus answered, 'Thou couldest have no power at all against me, except it were given thee from above: therefore he that delivered me unto thee hath the greater sin'" (John 19:11).

The death of Christ was a voluntary death. He laid down His life, not for His own benefit, but for His sheep. Jesus did not want them to suffer the cup of the wrath of God. He drank that Himself. "And he went a little further, and fell on his face, and prayed, saying, 'O my Father, if it be possible, let this cup pass from me: nevertheless not as I will, but as thou wilt'" (Matthew 26:39).

The sheep for whom Christ died are the ones whom the Father has given to Him. He knows them by name. "To him the porter openeth; and the sheep hear his voice: and he calleth his own sheep by name, and leadeth them out" (John 10:3). As Jesus knows His own, His sheep know Jesus.

They know His voice. "And other sheep I have, which are not of this fold: them also I must bring, and they shall hear my voice; and there shall be one fold, and one shepherd" (John 10:16).

They know His look. "And the Lord turned, and looked upon Peter. And Peter remembered the word of the Lord, how he had said unto him, 'Before the cock crow, thou shalt deny me thrice'" (Luke 22:61).

They know His nail scarred hands. "Then saith he to Thomas, 'Reach hither thy finger, and behold my hands; and reach hither thy hand, and thrust it into my side: and be not faithless, but believing.' And Thomas answered and said unto him, 'My Lord and my God'" (John 20:27).

They know His true identity. "He saith unto them, 'But whom say ye that I am?' And Simon Peter answered and said, 'Thou art the Christ, the Son of the living God'" (Matthew 16:15).

They know His doctrine. "And he said unto them, 'Unto you it is given to know the mystery of the kingdom of God: but unto them that are without, all these things are done in parables'" (Mark 4:11).

They know His love. "Now before the feast of the Passover, when Jesus knew that his hour was come that he should depart out of this world unto the Father, having loved his own which were in the world, he loved them unto the end" (John 13:1).

The sheep, whom Jesus loves, follow Him.

In contrast, the hireling, possibly a reference to the Pharisees and other Jewish religious leaders, will flee and leave the flock in time of trouble. "But he that is an hireling, and not the shepherd, whose own the sheep are not, seeth the wolf coming, and leaveth the sheep, and fleeth: and the wolf catcheth them, and scattereth the sheep. The hireling fleeth, because he is an hireling, and careth not for the sheep" (John 10:12–13).

The sheep which follow Christ consists of a large flock of Jews and Gentiles. As Peter was to minister to the circumcised, to Jews, Paul was to minister to the Gentiles. "Nevertheless, brethren, I have written the more boldly unto you in some sort, as putting you in mind, because of the grace that is given to me of God, that I should be the minister of Jesus Christ to the Gentiles, ministering the gospel of God, that the offering up of the Gentiles might be acceptable, being sanctified by the Holy Ghost" (Romans 15:15–16).

The ingathering of the Gentiles began in earnest with the giving of the Great Commission. The gospel is to go into all nations, even to the uttermost parts of the earth. "Go ye therefore, and teach all nations, baptizing them in the name of the Father, and of the Son, and of the Holy Ghost; teaching them to observe all things whatsoever I have commanded you: and, lo, I am with you alway, even unto the end of the world. Amen" (Matthew 28:19–20).

As the sheep know Christ, and as Christ knows His sheep, so the Father knows Jesus. There is an intimacy that is stressed. "As the Father knoweth me, even so know I the Father: and I lay down my life for the sheep" (John 10:15).

The sheep of Christ, consisting of Jew and Gentiles, form one fold with one shepherd, Jesus Christ. "And other sheep I have, which are not of this fold: them also I must bring, and they shall hear my voice; and there shall be one fold, and one shepherd" (John 10:16).

The Good Shepherd is also the Great Shepherd, for He has omnipotent power. He has the power to dismiss His spirit by laying down His life, and the power to take it again. "Therefore doth my Father love me, because I lay down my life, that I might take it again" (John 10:17).

The Good Shepherd, who is the Great Shepherd, is the Guiding Shepherd, for He has received a commandment from the Father to be the Bishop and Shepherd of the souls of the flock of God. "For ye were as sheep going astray; but are now returned unto the Shepherd and Bishop of your souls" (1 Peter 2:25).

The Good Shepherd, who is the Great Shepherd, who is the Guiding Shepherd, is the Providing Shepherd, for He feeds His sheep, and tells others to do the same. Those who love Christ will feed His sheep. "So when they had dined, Jesus saith to Simon Peter, 'Simon, son of Jonas, lovest thou me more than these?' He saith unto him, 'Yea, Lord; thou knowest that I love thee.' He saith unto him, 'Feed my lambs.' He saith to him again the second time, 'Simon, son of Jonas, lovest thou me?' He saith unto him, 'Yea, Lord; thou knowest that I love thee.' He saith unto him, 'Feed my sheep.' He saith unto him the third time, 'Simon, son of Jonas, lovest thou me?' Peter was grieved because he said unto him the third time, 'Lovest thou me?' And he said unto him, 'Lord, thou knowest all things; thou knowest that I love thee.' Jesus saith unto him, 'Feed my sheep'" (John 21:15–17).

The result of the revelation about Jesus was a division among the Jews. "There was a division therefore again among the Jews for these sayings" (John 10:19). Many people thought Jesus had a demon, was mentally insane, and should not be listened to. "And many of them said, 'He hath a devil, and is mad; why hear ye him?'" (John 10:20). Others wisely discerned that Jesus could not possibly be demon possessed, because a demon cannot perform a miracle. A demon cannot make the blind to see. "Others said, 'These are not the words of him that hath a devil. Can a devil open the eyes of the blind?'" (John 10:21).

Christ makes the blind to see, physically and spiritually, for He is the Good Shepherd.

9

I AM *the Resurrection*

After the death of Lazarus, Jesus visited the home of Mary and Martha where He declared that He was the resurrection. "Jesus said unto her, 'I am the resurrection, and the life: he that believeth in me, though he were dead, yet shall he live'" (John 11:25).

The context for this statement begins with the illness of Lazarus. A notice was sent to Jesus that the one whom He loved was sick. "Therefore his sisters sent unto him, saying, 'Lord, behold, he whom thou lovest is sick.' When Jesus heard that, he said, 'This sickness is not unto death, but for the glory of God, that the Son of God might be glorified thereby'" (John 11:3–4).

The Lord's response to the news was encouraging. Then, Jesus did something that was not expected. He delayed going to the home of His friend, whom He loved, for two days. "Now Jesus loved Martha, and her sister, and Lazarus. When he had heard therefore that he was sick, he abode two days still in the same place where he was. Then after that saith he to his disciples, 'Let us go into Judaea again.' His disciples say unto him, 'Master, the Jews of late sought to stone thee; and goest thou thither again?'" (John 11:5–8).

Jesus did not do the expected. He did not do what Mary and Martha expected Him to do. Jesus did not do what His disciples expected Him to do, and that was to stay away from Judea. Addressing the disciples first, Jesus explained why He would return to Judea. "Jesus answered, 'Are there not twelve hours in the day? If any man walk in the day, he stumbleth not, because he seeth the light of this world. But if a man walk in the night, he stumbleth, because there is no light in him.' These things said he: and after that he saith unto them, 'Our friend Lazarus sleepeth; but I go, that I may awake him out of sleep'" (John 11:9–11). Upon hearing the concern of His disciples, Jesus used the moment to teach a spiritual truth. Simply enough, there was work to do, and so the work must begin immediately.

It was no doubt early in the morning when Jesus told His disciples they would return to Judea, because the practical illustration Jesus used was the twelve hours of work allowed in the day by the light of the sun. Jesus said that it is better to walk and work in the day, because in the night, a person might stumble.

While the disciples were meditating on the spiritual message the Lord had concerning walking and working in the light, Jesus said to them something else they did not fully comprehend. "Our friend Lazarus sleepeth."

By calling Lazarus, "our friend", Jesus was conveying an important concept. Our friends should be the friends of Jesus. Far too many Christians are unduly influenced by people who are not friends of Jesus. A non-Christian parent will try to influence the children not to go to Sunday school or church. A non-Christian friend will often influence a Christian not to walk with the Lord and engage in spiritual work.

Because the disciples did not understand the words of Jesus, they said something that made perfect sense to them. If Lazarus was sleeping, he should do well to rest. "Then said his disciples, 'Lord, if he sleep, he shall do well'" (John 11:12).

However, Jesus was not speaking about physical rest for their friend Lazarus. The Lord was speaking of His death. There is a spiritual language of the heart that every Christian must learn in order to be spiritually discerning. "Howbeit Jesus spake of his death: but they thought that he had spoken of taking of rest in sleep. Then said Jesus unto them plainly, 'Lazarus is dead'" (John 11:13–14).

While the disciples contemplated the force of that shocking statement, Jesus continued to speak in cryptic, but spiritual language, by saying He was glad (*chairo*). Jesus said He was cheerful, or calmly happy, He was not there at the death of their friend Lazarus. "And I am glad for your sakes that I was not there, to the intent ye may believe; nevertheless let us go unto him" (John 11:15).

From a human perspective, the disciples might have interpreted the words of Jesus to mean that He was glad He was not present to see the painful demise of a beloved friend. From a divine perspective, what Jesus meant was, "I am glad I was not there for your sake, because, you have seen nothing yet of the glory that is soon to come when I bring Lazarus back from the dead." A lesson is learned. Every event in life can be viewed from either a human, or a divine perspective. The difference will make the heart sad, or glad.

Setting aside what Jesus might have meant by saying He was glad, the disciples did comprehend the Lord's determination to return to Judea. The Lord said with firmness, "Let us go unto him." Hearing that, Thomas thought Jesus meant that they would all return to Judea in order to die. "Then said Thomas, which is called Didymus, unto his fellow disciples, 'Let us also go, that we may die with him'" (John 11:16).

It could not have been a happy journey the disciples of Jesus were making with their Master. They were in a state of emotional shock upon hearing that their friend, who they thought was sick and resting, was dead. They were perplexed by the decision of Jesus to return to harm's way. They were convinced they too were going to suffer arrest, and die. To go to Bethany was to go near Jerusalem, the source of much hostility to the public ministry of Christ. To their eternal credit, the disciples went to Judea with Jesus. "Then when Jesus came, he found that he had lain in the grave four days already. Now Bethany was nigh unto Jerusalem, about fifteen furlongs off: and many of the Jews came to Martha and Mary, to comfort them concerning their brother. Then Martha, as soon as she heard that Jesus was coming, went and met him: but Mary sat still in the house. Then said Martha unto Jesus, 'Lord, if thou hadst been here, my brother had not died'" (John 11:17–21).

Upon arriving at the home of Mary and Martha in Bethany, Jesus and His disciples found that Lazarus had been dead for four days. In the Jewish culture, that notation by John is significant. Many Jews at this time in history believed that when a person died, their spirit would return to visit the body until the fourth day. After that, even the most hopeful Jew relinquished any hope the body might revive. Lazarus was dead. He had been dead for four days with the decaying process begun.

Jesus and His disciples also found many people gathered who had come to comfort Martha. However, Martha was not ready to be comforted. There was bitterness in her heart toward Jesus. "Lord, if thou hadst been here, my brother had not died."

Martha's statement was not fair or true. She did not know what the Lord would have allowed. She did not know what God was willing to do under different circumstances. It is not wise to speak with certainty about things that are beyond our control. Much anger is generated when something is postulated, and then asserted as if that is the reality.

Martha is not to be commended for her assertion. It was presumptuous, and a public rebuke of the Lord of glory. It was a shameful comment because of something else. Martha did not know what the Lord would do. She did not foresee the resurrection of her brother. Had Martha said, "Lord, I am so glad you are here. I believe that, even though my brother has died, you are able to raise Him now, and I humbly ask you to do that." Had Martha expressed her faith in the future, then the moment would reflect her spiritual maturity. When the Lord blesses, it is easy to have faith. It is when the goodness of God is veiled, that spiritual maturity is tested.

With that gentle rebuke against Martha, her next expression is encouraging. "But I know, that even now, whatsoever thou wilt ask of God, God will give it thee" (John 11:22).

If these words express hope that Jesus would do something special, then the faith of Martha is vindicated. Sometimes, after an angry outburst, the heart wants to make amends for being too harsh. There is no reason to believe that Martha expected an immediate resurrection miracle, for her interaction with Jesus does not indicate that, though her heart must have been comforted with the promise of Jesus. "Jesus saith unto her, 'Thy brother shall rise again'" (John 11:23).

Perhaps still on an emotional roller coaster, Martha responded. "Martha saith unto him, 'I know that he shall rise again in the resurrection at the last day'" (John 11:24).

As a rule, people do not like to be told something they already know very well. It appears to be condescending. Also, people do not like meaningless platitudes, especially in times of emotional duress and stress.

We do not know the tone of Martha's response to Jesus, whether it was an affirmation of her own faith, or an irritation that Jesus would state what a faithful Jew already believed, namely, there is to be a bodily resurrection of the dead at the last day. In her belief, Martha was conservative. Not everyone in Israel believed in a future resurrection. The Pharisees did, but the Sadducees rejected the doctrine of the resurrection of the dead. What is certain is that Martha was not looking for an immediate resurrection. She did have faith in a future resurrection on the last day.

The response of Jesus to Martha's statement is one of the grandest statements every uttered. "Jesus said unto her, 'I am the resurrection, and the life: he that believeth in me, though he were dead, yet shall he live; and whosoever liveth and believeth in me shall never die...'" (John 11:25–26).

Jesus does not say, "I Am the One who will raise Lazarus." Jesus says something far more profound. Jesus says, "I Am the resurrection, and the life." Jesus is the One who not only gives light to the world, He is the Light of the world. Jesus not only helps people through the door to safety and eternal life, He is the Door. Jesus not only gives life, He is Life. Jesus not only raises people from the dead, He is the resurrection.

In the culture of the day, if a characteristic was closely associated with a particular person, that person could, in terms of speech patterns, be identified with that characteristic. For example, God is love. Therefore, love is God.

In context, Jesus is so united with power, and the power over death, that it could be said He is the resurrection. By affirming He is the resurrection, Jesus was definitively answering the question of antiquity uttered by Job. "If a man dies, shall he live again?" (Job 14:14).

Job's question has been in the mind of every human being since death was first experienced. In every culture, tribe, and civilization, people speculate about death and the afterlife. People want to know, "When I die, is that the end?" People are anxious to know if the totality of personal existence is summed up between the two points of birth and death. Or, is there something more?

For most people, life is so precious there beats within the heart a hope that there will be life beyond the grave. When Plato wrote about the death of Socrates, he gave a philosophical argument for the immortality of the soul. There is an argument for life after death borrowed from the cyclical character seen in nature. Something is born, it grows to maturity, it lives, it dies, and it becomes the source for new life. When something dies, it becomes a metamorphosis for another way of living. Paul spoke about different kinds of life, and different bodies for each life. There is a body suited for the spirit world. The ancient Egyptians, long before the Greeks believed that the soul, or Ba, survived death of the physical body. An image from The Egyptian Book of the Dead conveys the idea of the transmigration of the soul, or reincarnation.

The greatest hope that humans have is found in the historical resurrection of Jesus Christ. The resurrection of Jesus is the first among the resurrection of many. Jesus was resurrected for us that we might also participate in His life.

One of the reasons why first century Christians were so willing to undergo martyrdom is because they believed in the resurrection of Jesus. They were convinced the grave was not the final dimension. Instead of death being the bitter victory for Satan, death is an entrance into eternal life. The victory belongs to Christ. Death has been defeated. Death, for the Christian, is a transition to a better environment. All of this comes down, not to a debate, but to a person. The only question is, "Do you believe?" "Do you believe Jesus when He says, 'He that believeth in me, though he were dead, yet shall he live: and whosoever liveth and believeth in me shall never die...?'"

At first, these words sound contradictory. Jesus said that a dead person can live. Then He said that a person who believes in Him shall never die. What Jesus is saying is that there is a sense in which people who believe in Him never die. In another sense people do die. Physically, people die. People must prepare to meet God.

In another sense, the soul that trusts in Jesus shall never die the death of the wicked which is eternal separation from God. The *"zoe"*, or the life which Jesus gives to His people begins the moment faith is born in the heart. Zoe life cannot be killed by death. Physical death cannot destroy the life that Christ puts into the believer.

The day that the body of a believer dies is not the day that self dies. That is the day a person becomes more conscious of reality. That is why Paul was ambivalent about living, and dying. "For I am in a strait betwixt two, having a desire to depart, and to be with Christ; which is far better" (Philippians 1:23).

As Jesus was comforting Martha, He was conveying to her that He was not just talking about a future resurrection. She was talking to the One who was the resurrection. Then, Jesus asked Martha a question. "... Believest thou this?" (John 11:26).

Before man was put in the Garden of Eden, God has asked His creation to believe Him. Lucifer and many angels did not believe God and were cast out of heaven. Adam and Eve stopped believing God, and ate of the forbidden fruit. Jesus asked people to believe in Him, and for this reason. A person's honor is bound up in what they say. The character of God cannot be divorced from His Word. If He has spoken, it must be true. Sin has destroyed the soul of man, reflected in the constant perversion of individuals.

An internet headline for April 16, 2016, read, "My Husband is now My Wife". The militant homosexual and transgendered community finds new ways to express its agenda. This is done because life, and that more abundantly, is pursued outside of Christ. A life without God is pursued because people do not believe the Lord. In grace, the Holy Spirit changes the hearts of many who do believe in Jesus. Martha was one such person. "She saith unto him, 'Yea, Lord: I believe that thou art the Christ, the Son of God, which should come into the world'" (John 11:27).

Martha said, "Yes, Lord, I do believe." With that she turned, and went into the house to get Mary. Her private conversation with Jesus, overheard by the disciples, was finished. Now, others must hear the good news. Martha must find Mary. "And when she had so said, she went her way, and called Mary her sister secretly, saying, 'The Master is come, and calleth for thee'" (John 11:28).

When Mary came to Jesus, she bowed before Him in honor, only to make the same charge as Martha had made. "Then when Mary was come where Jesus was, and saw him, she fell down at his feet, saying unto him, 'Lord, if thou hadst been here, my brother had not died'" (John 11:32).

Rather than review what He had said to Martha, Jesus, being grieved in His own spirit, simply asked where the body was laid. Then, Jesus wept.

Some of the people who had come to comfort the sisters noticed the tears of Jesus. Others wondered out loud why Jesus had not used His known healing powers to keep Lazarus from dying.

Finally, the procession arrived at the cave where Lazarus was buried. A stone had been rolled over the entrance. Jesus stood before the grave site, and said, "Take ye away the stone," only to hear the voice of doubt from Martha. She did not fully understand after all what Jesus had been saying. ". . . Lord, by

I AM the Resurrection

this time he stinketh: for he hath been dead four days" (John 11:39).

The physical decay of Lazarus speaks of the spiritual decay of every unbeliever who is dead in trespasses and sin. Such a person, in the sight of God, "stinketh". Nevertheless, God still works a work of grace in the soul of those who are offensive to Him. Jesus answered Martha's protest with a gentle rebuke. "Jesus saith unto her, 'Said I not unto thee, that, if thou wouldest believe, thou shouldest see the glory of God?'" (John 11:40).

With those words, the debate was over, and there was obedience. The stone was removed, and then Jesus offered a prayer. "Then they took away the stone from the place where the dead was laid. And Jesus lifted up his eyes, and said, 'Father, I thank thee that thou hast heard me. And I knew that thou hearest me always: but because of the people which stand by I said it, that they may believe that thou hast sent me'" (John 11:41).

After He had finished praying, Jesus cried with a loud voice, and spoke to Lazarus, a man four days dead. "And when he thus had spoken, he cried with a loud voice, 'Lazarus, come forth'" (John 11:43).

The physical resurrection of Lazarus is a perfect illustration of the spiritual resurrection of every soul. Salvation is personal. Salvation is a sovereign act of God. Salvation is apart from human merit or ability. Regeneration is the mighty work of the Holy Spirit. Only God can create life. Only God can recreate life. Salvation is by divine selection. Salvation is God showing mercy to one, but not to all without exception. Only Lazarus was raised from the dead. Life is created, and recreated, by the power of the divine call. By His word, all that is created is.

The same way Jesus shouted, "Lazarus, come forth," is the same way He created the universe. He spoke, and it was done. "And he that was dead came forth, bound hand and foot with grave clothes, and his face was bound about with a napkin. Jesus saith unto them, 'Loose him, and let him go'" (John 11:44).

The result of the miracle of Jesus was that people believed. "Then many of the Jews which came to Mary, and had seen the things which Jesus did, believed on him" (John 11:45).

The people had a right to be astonished, because Jesus has the key, the power to unlock the grave.

Now, the question comes to you personally, "Do you believe?"

10

I AM the Way, the Truth, and the Life

"Jesus saith unto him, 'I am the way, the truth, and the life: no man cometh unto the Father, but by me'" (John 14:6).

Jesus was going away, and His disciples did not fully understand. Certainly, they did not want Jesus to leave them. Nevertheless, Jesus was going away. On the night before His death, in the Upper Room, Jesus gave a discourse. In order to prepare the hearts of His disciples, Jesus began by saying that their hearts should not be discouraged. "Let not your heart be troubled: ye believe in God, believe also in me" (John

14:1). The same confidence the disciples had in God was to be placed in Christ.

Then, Jesus revealed something wonderful about heaven. In heaven there are many dwelling places. If that were not the truth, Jesus would have told them something else. "In my Father's house are many mansions: if it were not so, I would have told you. I go to prepare a place for you" (John 14:2).

Jesus went on to say that He was going to go to His Father's house in order to prepare a place for His disciples. Then, He would return to them so that where He goes, they can be with Him forever and forever. "And whither I go ye know, and the way ye know" (John 14:4).

To further encourage and comfort His disciples, Jesus reminded them of two facts. First, they already knew where Jesus was going. Second, they already knew the way to where Jesus was going.

That is a refreshing statement. Sometimes people do not know, what they do not know. Sometimes people are ignorant, and do not know they are ignorant. The Pharisees did not know spiritual truth. They did not know that Jesus was the Christ, the Son of God. They did not know they were spiritually blind.

Sometimes people do not know, what they do know. That seems like a contradiction, but it is the truth. People know something, but they have a lapse of memory. They need to be reminded of what they have previously learned. Jesus had taught the disciples many wonderful truths. Now, He was reminding them of what they knew. They knew that heaven is for real. They knew that Jesus is the Door to heaven. He is The Way to have access to God. This was taught to them in John 10.

Frustrated with what Jesus was saying, Thomas disputed the statement of Jesus saying, "Lord, we know not whither thou goest; and how can we know the way?" (John 14:5). It is always wrong to contradict the Lord Jesus Christ. It is always wrong to correct the Lord of Glory. Thomas was wrong to speak on behalf of the disciples, and say, "Lord, we do not know where you are going, so how can we possibly know the way?"

In matchless tender grace and patience, Jesus responded to Thomas. He did not respond with sharp words of rebuke, but with additional information. "Thomas," Jesus said, "I am the way, the truth, and the life: no man cometh unto the Father, but by me" (John 14:6).

Perhaps at that moment, the Holy Spirit reminded Thomas of what he knew. Thomas might have remembered the truth that Jesus is the Sheep-Gate by which the flock of God enters into the sheepfold. Jesus was not saying anything new here. He was simply reminding the disciples that He was The Way to God. Once more, there is no pluralism allowed in the words of Jesus. The Lord does not offer many ways to heaven. He alone is The Way.

The Lord went on to say, "Thomas, if ye had known me, you should have known my Father also: and from henceforth ye know him, and have seen Him" (John 14:7). When Jesus told Thomas that from now on he would know the Father, and see Him, the curiosity of Philip was aroused. Wanting to enter into the conversation, Philip, who had been listening to the exchange between Jesus and Thomas, spoke, and said unto Jesus, "Lord, shew us the Father, and it sufficeth us" (John 14:8). The word sufficeth means it will be sufficient. However, Philip was showing how shallow he, and the other disciples were, in understanding spiritual truth.

For several years Philip, and the disciples, had watched Jesus turn water into wine. They had seen Him raise the dead. They had watched as the blind were made to see. They beheld the wisdom of the Lord as He responded to the Pharisees, and still were not satisfied. They wanted one more thing. They wanted to see the Father. The disciples wanted to see what even Moses was denied, and of which every person has been denied since Adam and Eve were banished from Paradise. They wanted to see the invisible God. Just once. Show us the Father, and we will be satisfied.

The heart of Philip was beating very rapidly now, for the heart of humanity longs to see God. The making of idols reflects man's longing to see God in some form. Moses wanted to see God, but was told that it was impossible. "And he said, 'Thou canst not see my face: for there shall no man see me, and live'" (Exodus 33:20). The Gospel of John affirms that no one has seen God at any time. "No man hath seen God at any time; the only begotten Son, which is in the bosom of the Father, he hath declared him" (John 1:18).

There are reasons why God the Father cannot be seen.

God is holy, and man is unholy. Exodus 3:5, "And he said, 'Draw not nigh hither: put off thy shoes from off thy feet, for the place whereon thou standest is holy ground.'"

God is light, and man is full of darkness. 1 John 1:5, "This then is the message which we have heard of him, and declare unto you, that God is light, and in him is no darkness at all."

God is Spirit. His essential nature is spirit. John 4:24, "God is a Spirit: and they that worship Him must worship Him in spirit and in truth."

While God cannot be fully seen, He can be known. What God has done in matchless grace is to allow His creation to see His veiled glory. Moses saw something of God, but He did not see God Himself fully. "And the Lord said unto Moses, 'I will do this thing also that thou hast spoken: for thou hast found grace in my sight, and I know thee by name.' And he said, 'I beseech thee, show me thy glory.' And he said, 'I will make all my goodness pass before thee, and I will proclaim the name of the Lord before thee; and will be gracious to whom I will be gracious, and will show mercy on whom I will show mercy.' And he said, 'Thou canst not see my face: for there shall no man see me, and live.' And the Lord said, 'Behold, there is a place by me, and thou shalt stand upon a rock: and it shall come to pass, while my glory passeth by, that I will put thee in a cleft of the rock, and will cover thee with my hand while I pass by: and I will take away mine hand, and thou shalt see my back parts: but my face shall not be seen'" (Exodus 13:17–23).

Again, in matchless grace, in order to allow His creation to see His veiled glory, God the Father, in the person of His Son, Jesus Christ, has revealed Himself. This is what Jesus meant when He responded to Philip. "Jesus saith unto him, 'Have I been so long time with you, and yet hast thou not known me, Philip? He that hath seen me hath seen the Father; and how sayest thou then, Show us the Father?'" (John 14:9).

Perhaps the Lord was exasperated when He said to Philip, "Have I spent all of this time with you, and yet you still do not know me?" What more did Jesus have to do to convince the disciples that He was Immanuel, God with them? Did Philip not remember the words of the prophet Isaiah? "For unto us a child is born, unto us a son is given: and the government shall be upon his shoulder: and his name shall be called Wonderful, Counsellor, The mighty God, The everlasting Father, The Prince of Peace" (Isaiah 9:6).

To see Christ is to see the Father, but it is not to see the Father fully. In Christ all the manifestation of the divinity of the Father is fully expressed, but still, that is not to see the Father. "For in him dwelleth all the fullness of the Godhead bodily" (Colossians 2:9).

"Philip, you are talking to God incarnate. You are witnessing the expression of the Godhead bodily. You are talking to the expressed image of the person who is divine. You can behold the visible manifestation of the invisible God. You have seen Me, Philip. You have seen the Father."

The words of Jesus to Philip are one of the most fantastic claims Jesus made. Once more Jesus was claiming to be very God, of very God. The idea that Jesus never made any claims to deity is absurd. Indeed He did, and the Jews took up stones to kill Him for claiming to be God, for that was the proper punishment for blasphemy (Leviticus 24:16).

The claim of Jesus to be God is recorded in John 10:30, "Jesus said, 'I and my Father are one.'" Those who heard Jesus speak understood what He meant, and took up stones to stone Him. "Jesus answered them, 'Many good works have I showed you from my Father; for which of those works do ye stone me?' The Jews answered him, saying, 'For a good work we stone thee not; but for blasphemy; and because that thou, being a man, makest thyself God'" (John 10:32–33).

The claim of Jesus to be God is found in John 8:58, "Jesus said unto them, 'Verily, verily, I say unto you, before Abraham was, I am.'" Once more the Jews attempted to stone Jesus. "Then they took up stones to cast at him: but Jesus hid himself, and went out of the temple, going through the midst of them, and so passed by" (John 8:59).

The claim of Jesus to be God is found in John 14:9, "Jesus saith unto him, 'Have I been so long time with you, and yet hast thou not known me, Philip? He that hath seen me hath seen the Father; and how sayest thou then, Show us the Father?'"

Certainly, the disciples of Christ were convinced that Jesus was God. "And Thomas answered and said unto him, 'My Lord and my God'" (John 20:28).

The authors of Scripture were convinced that Jesus was divine.

John said that the Word was God, and dwelt among us. "In the beginning was the Word, and the Word was with God, and the Word was God. . . . And the Word was made flesh, and dwelt among us, (and we beheld his glory, the glory as of the only begotten of the Father,) full of grace and truth" (John 1:1; 1:14).

Luke recorded how Paul preached that God purchased His church with His own blood. "Take heed therefore unto yourselves, and to all the flock, over the which the Holy Ghost hath made you overseers, to feed the church of God, which he hath purchased with his own blood" (Acts 20:28).

Referring to Jesus, Paul wrote of God our Savior. "Looking for that blessed hope, and the glorious appearing of the great God and our Savior Jesus Christ" (Titus 2:13).

The author of Hebrews wrote of Jesus as God. "But unto the Son he saith, 'Thy throne, O God, is for ever and ever: a scepter of righteousness is the scepter of thy kingdom'" (Hebrews 1:8).

Jesus has to be God, for only God could pay the infinite penalty for sin against God, and then forgive sinners. "And the scribes and the Pharisees began to reason, saying, 'Who is this which speaketh blasphemies? Who can forgive sins, but God alone?'" (Luke 5:21). "For he hath made him to be sin for us, who knew no sin; that we might be made the righteousness of God in him" (2 Corinthians 5:21). "And he is the propitiation for our sins: and not for ours only, but also for the sins of the whole world" (1 John 2:2).

There is such a unity in the Godhead, that to see the Son, is to see the Father. That is what Jesus was telling Phillip. The hearts of those, who believe Christ, rejoice. If you know the Son, you know the Father. To believe in Jesus, is to believe in the Father. Conversely, the same is true. If you know the Father, you will know the Son. If you see the Father, you will see the Son. To believe in the Father, is to believe in the Son.

"I can of mine own self do nothing: as I hear, I judge: and my judgment is just; because I seek not mine own will, but the will of the Father which hath sent me. If I bear witness of myself, my witness is not true. There is another that beareth witness of me; and I know that the witness which he witnesseth of me is true. Ye sent unto John, and he bare witness unto the truth. But I receive not testimony from man: but these things I say, that ye might be saved. He was a burning and a shining light: and ye were willing for a season to rejoice in his light. But I have greater witness than that of John: for the works which the Father hath given me to finish, the same works that I do, bear witness of me, that the Father hath sent me. And the

Father himself, which hath sent me, hath borne witness of me. Ye have neither heard his voice at any time, nor seen his shape" (John 5:30–37). "I am one that bear witness of myself, and the Father that sent me beareth witness of me" (John 8:18). The way to the Father is through the Son. The way to see the Father, is to see the Son.

As Jesus is the Way, so He is the Truth. "Jesus saith unto him, 'I am the way, the truth, and the life: no man cometh unto the Father, but by me'" (John 14:6). Though many are skeptical of truth, and ask in mockery with Pilate, "What is truth?" Jesus did believe in ultimate truth, and claimed that He is the source of all truth.

There are several ways to confirm that Jesus is the truth.

The Old Testament. The Bible speaks of Christ. "Search the scriptures; for in them ye think ye have eternal life: and they are they which testify of me. And ye will not come to me, that ye might have life" (John 5:39–40).

His sinlessness. "Which of you convinceth me of sin? And if I say the truth, why do ye not believe me?" (John 8:46).

He spoke without error. "And when he had thus spoken, one of the officers which stood by struck Jesus with the palm of his hand, saying, 'Answerest thou the high priest so?' Jesus answered him, 'If I have spoken evil, bear witness of the evil: but if well, why smitest thou me?'" (John 18:22–23).

Jesus prefaced all of His remarks by saying that what He taught was not His own teaching, but that of God. Furthermore, He would teach without error. Finally, He is the embodiment of all truth.

Either such claims of Jesus are the claims of a liar, who knows He is lying, an egotistical maniac, or the claims of an honest person who really is who He claimed to be, the Son of the Living God. Liberal scholars and nonbelievers are wrong to say that Jesus is a great Moral Teacher if in fact He erred in what He said, was delusional, or a lying charlatan. No Moral Teacher would make exalted claims about himself. Jesus taught with authority because He had self-awareness.

In the modern culture, truth is despised, even in the church. It is often said that doctrine is not important, but relationships are important. It is said that truth is relative. It is said that what is true for one person, may not be true for another person. For those who say doctrine is not important, but relationships are important, what is really being said is that this is truth: getting along. Here then is the logical fallacy of illogical reasoning. There must be an understanding of truth if an axiom is to be evaluated. To set relationships against truth is illogical.

It is the Word of God which defines truth. Jesus is the Word incarnate. Truth cannot be despised, without at the same time despising Christ, because He is the truth. If you want to know the truth, go to the source of truth, which is to say, go to Christ. Go now. Go quickly. Go without delay. To go to Christ is to have life, eternal life. "And I give unto them eternal life; and they shall never perish, neither shall any man pluck them out of my hand" (John 10:28).

11

I AM the True Vine

Each of the "I AM" statements in Scripture uttered by Christ is preceded by the "*ego emi*" of the Septuagint for God's sacred name, Yahweh, "I AM who I AM." The seventh "I AM" of Christ is given in John 15.

"I am the true vine, and my Father is the husbandman. Every branch in me that beareth not fruit he taketh away: and every branch that beareth fruit, he purgeth it, that it may bring forth more fruit. Now ye are clean through the word which I have spoken unto you. Abide in me, and I in you. As the branch cannot bear fruit of itself, except it abide in the vine; no more can ye, except ye abide in me. I am the vine, ye are the branches: He that abideth in me, and I in him, the same bringeth forth much fruit: for without me ye can do nothing" (John 15:1–5).

In this passage, Jesus says that He is the "True Vine" in verse 1, and the "Vine" in verse 5. This may be a difference without a distinction, or it may be significant. In the statement about Himself, Jesus also speaks of the productivity of His disciples. They must bear fruit. Spiritual fruit is possible only by remaining closely united to Christ, as branches are connected to the vine.

By saying that He was the True Vine, Jesus was placing Himself in contrast with the false vine, or the corrupt vine. Those who heard Jesus speak understood what He was saying, because the metaphor of the vine was not something new to those listening. The image of the vine was used in the Old Testament to describe the relationship between God and Israel.

"Give ear, O Shepherd of Israel, thou that leadest Joseph like a flock; thou that dwellest between the cherubims, shine forth. Before Ephraim and Benjamin and Manasseh stir up thy strength, and come and save us. Turn us again, O God, and cause thy face to shine; and we shall be saved. O Lord God of hosts, how long wilt thou be angry against the prayer of thy people? Thou feedest them with the bread of tears; and givest them tears to drink in great measure. Thou makest us a strife unto our neighbors: and our enemies laugh among themselves" (Psalm 80:1–6).

God is spoken of as being the Shepherd of Israel, as Jesus said He was the Good Shepherd. As the Shepherd God, He dwelt between the cherubims, a reference to the Ark of the Covenant where the cherubims guarded the Mercy Seat in the Holy of Holies.

The Psalmist is weeping before God because Israel was experiencing God's judgment upon the nation. God had given them "bread for tears." The prayer is for God to restore His people to favor. The petition to be turned is repeated in verse 7.

"Turn us again, O God of hosts, and cause thy face to shine; and we shall be saved. Thou hast brought a vine out of Egypt: thou hast cast out the heathen, and planted it. Thou preparedst room before it, and didst cause it to take deep root, and it filled the land. The hills were covered with the shadow of it, and the boughs thereof were like the goodly cedars. She sent out her boughs unto the sea, and her branches unto the river. Why hast thou then broken down her hedges, so that all they which pass by the way do pluck her? The boar out of the wood doth waste it, and the wild beast of the field doth devour it" (Psalm 80:7–13).

The Psalmist remembers the history of Israel. Israel was like a vine brought out of Egypt by God, and planted among the heathen. The Lord caused it to take deep root so that it grew and filled the land. The growth of the vine was spectacular, for it covered the hills. Roots forming new branches were sent out in all directions. Then, suddenly, judgment came. God broke down the hedges which protected the vine. The vine became subject to the will of any stranger to pluck and plunder its fruit. Wild animals came to waste the good vine. God was no longer protecting the vine. A plea is made for the Vinedresser to return to the vine to protect it.

"Return, we beseech thee, O God of hosts: look down from heaven, and behold, and visit this vine; and the vineyard which thy right hand hath planted, and the branch that thou madest strong for thyself. It is burned with fire, it is cut down: they perish at the rebuke of thy countenance. Let thy hand be upon the man of thy right hand, upon the son of man whom thou madest strong for thyself. So will not we go back from thee: quicken us, and we will call upon thy name. Turn us again, O Lord God of hosts, cause thy face to shine; and we shall be saved" (Psalm 80:14–19).

The Psalmist pleads with God to bring spiritual renewal to Israel by causing the people to turn to the Lord. The Psalmist recognizes what the vine cannot do, what the people of Israel cannot do. The vine cannot cure, or sanctify itself. It cannot protect itself. The vine is helpless and hopeless, unless God does something. Only if God acts will the vine, and thus the people of Israel, be saved.

The reference to the vineyard, "which thy right hand hath planted," could refer to the nation of Israel itself. It could also refer to David, or, ultimately, the Messiah. The plea in this prayer is for God to return to the vineyard, to save the vineyard He has planted.

Another illustration of Israel as the vine is found in the prophet Isaiah.

"Now will I sing to my well-beloved a song of my beloved touching his vineyard. My well-beloved hath a vineyard in a very fruitful hill: and he fenced it, and gathered out the stones thereof, and planted it with the choicest vine, and built a tower in the midst of it, and also made a winepress therein: and he looked that it should bring forth grapes, and it brought forth wild grapes. And now, O inhabitants of Jerusalem, and men of Judah, judge, I pray you, betwixt me and my vineyard. What could have been done more to my vineyard that I have not done in it? Wherefore, when I looked that it should bring forth grapes, brought it forth wild grapes? And now go to; I will tell you what I will do to my vineyard: I will take away the hedge thereof, and it shall be eaten up; and break down the wall thereof, and it shall be trodden down: and I will lay it waste: it shall not be pruned, nor dug; but there shall come up briers and thorns: I will also command the clouds that they rain no rain upon it. For the vineyard of the Lord of hosts is the house of Israel, and the men of Judah his pleasant plant: and he looked for judgment, but behold oppression; for righteousness, but behold a cry" (Isaiah 5:1–7).

Because the vineyard had become corrupt, God was determined to express His wrath against that which He planted. Specifically, the house of Israel and the men of Judah would be judged because God found no justice, no mercy, and no righteousness in the land. God expected fruit, but He found wild grapes. In the sight of God, Israel had become the corrupt vine.

Later, Jesus would contrast Himself with the corrupt vine, and declare that He was the True Vine. He was just. He was merciful. He was righteous. His Father was the Vinedresser. Jesus was saying that He was the embodiment of Israel.

The identity of Jesus to Israel is found elsewhere in Scripture, beginning with His infancy and early childhood. The Christ child is the embodiment of all that took place in the Old Testament whereby the people of God had to flee to Egypt, before they were delivered and brought to a Land of Promise, flowing with milk and honey.

"And being warned of God in a dream that they should not return to Herod, they departed into their own country another way. And when they were departed, behold, the angel of the Lord appeareth to Joseph in a dream, saying, 'Arise, and take the young child and his mother, and flee into Egypt, and be thou there until I bring thee word: for Herod will seek the young child to destroy him.' When he arose, he took the young child and his mother by night, and departed into Egypt: and was there until the death of Herod: that it might be fulfilled which was spoken of the Lord by the prophet, saying, 'Out of Egypt have I called my so'" (Matthew 2:12–15).

Jesus is so representative of His people, that He is Israel. Another cryptic reference conveying the Lord's identification with Israel is found in the opening chapter of John's Gospel, where the author says that the Word which became flesh, dwelt, or tabernacled, or pitched His tent in the midst of Israel. The allusion would have been to the Tabernacle in the Wilderness, which was a tent pitched in the middle of the camp. "And the Word was made flesh, and dwelt among us, (and we beheld his glory, the glory as of the only begotten of the Father,) full of grace and truth" (John 1:14).

In John 15, Jesus began His discourse by saying He was the True Vine, Israel. However, unlike the corrupt Israel, He would bring forth the good fruit, not the wild grapes. A True Vine will bring forth good fruit, because the Vinedresser is careful to attend to it.

If a vineyard is allowed to grow without being pruned, eventually, the harvest will be minimized. It is very important that the vines be pruned on a regular basis. This is true even for the branches which are fruit bearing. The flow of the sap is increased when careful pruning takes place.

Normally, every vine will have branches that die. The vinedresser will come to cut off the dead branches. The dead branches have no value, and so are burned. The dead branches have to be removed. The spiritual point of this narrative is that Jesus is teaching something about the church. The church is made up of sheep and goats, wheat and tares, and dead branches. There are people who are united with the church outwardly for a variety of reasons, but they are not truly converted, just like in the Old Testament expression of the church in Israel. In biblical language, "not all Israel is Israel." "Not as though the word of God hath taken none effect. For they are not all Israel, which are of Israel" (Romans 9:6).

Because the church is not pure, she needs a Good Shepherd to protect the flock from the wolves. The church needs a Gardener to root out the tares. The church needs a Vinedresser to prune the dead branches. There are people in the church who are like dead wood. They are like clouds that promise rain, but give no water. John 15 is not discussing Christians who do not bear fruit, because there are no Christians who do not bear fruit.

Not bearing fruit is a clear indication that a person is not a believer. They are dead wood, trying to attach themselves to the living True Vine. It is not going to happen. God will cut such a person off. "Every branch in me that beareth not fruit he taketh away" (John 15:2).

There are other people in the church, who have been made clean by Christ, and they do bear spiritual fruit, but they too need pruning in order to be able to bear more fruit. ". . . and every branch that beareth fruit, he purgeth it, that it may bring forth more fruit" (John 15:2). The branch has to be connected to the vine for the fruit to grow. Jesus is saying that He is the True Vine. His disciples must abide in Him if they want to grow. Those who do abide in Christ will be pruned by the Father, who is the Vinedresser, but that pruning process is fine. It will result in greater spiritual production.

To be productive as a Christian, a person must stay close to Christ. This is determined by several factors, such as how much time is spent in His Word, how much time is spent in communion, meditation, and prayer, how often the heart thinks about Jesus, whether or not spiritual songs are sung, whether or not there is gospel obedience, and how often Christ is shared with others.

If there is no evidence of spiritual fruit, there is no evidence of spiritual life. If there is evidence of spiritual fruit, how much spiritual fruit is produced will depend on how close to the True Vine the branch remains. A barely attached branch to the True Vine will barely produce spiritual fruit. It is the will of the Lord that His people bear much fruit. That is glorifying to the Father. Fruit bearing is not something that Christians should diminish or neglect. While there is great comfort in the doctrine of eternal security, the believer finds a greater sense of security when there is evidence of spiritual fruit in their life. The Christian is not to live a life of wasted years.

> Have you wondered alone on life's pathway,
> Have you lived without love a life of tears,
> Have you searched for the gray hidden meaning,
> Or is your life filled with long wasted years.
>
> Wasted years wasted years, Oh how foolish,
> As you walk all in darkness and fears,
> Turn around, turn around God is calling,
> He's calling you from a life of wasted years.

Search for wisdom and seek understanding,
    There is someone who knows and always hears,
Give it up, give it up the load you are bearing,
    You can't go on in a life of wasted years.

Don't you know Jesus died for all sinners,
    He loves you and your guilt he gladly bears,
Come to Him, Come to Him your sin confessing,
    You can go on with a life of fruitful years.[4]

---

[4] Attributed to Walley Foley.

12

The Eighth "I AM"

Normally, there are seven "I AM" passages that are listed. But there should be eight.

I AM the Bread of Life. "And Jesus said unto them, I am the bread of life: he that cometh to me shall never hunger; and he that believeth on me shall never thirst" (John 6:35).

I AM the Light of the World. "Then spake Jesus again unto them, saying, 'I am the light of the world: he that followeth me shall not walk in darkness, but shall have the light of life'" (John 8:12).

I AM before Abraham. "Jesus said unto them, 'Verily, verily, I say unto you, before Abraham was, I am'" (John 8:58).

I AM the Door. "I am the door: by me if any man enter in, he shall be saved, and shall go in and out, and find pasture" (John 10:9).

I AM the Good Shepherd. "I am the good shepherd: the good shepherd giveth his life for the sheep" (John 10:11).

I AM the Resurrection and the Life. "Jesus said unto her, 'I am the resurrection, and the life: he that believeth in me, though he were dead, yet shall he live: and whosoever liveth and believeth in me shall never die. Believest thou this?'" (John 11:25–26).

I AM the Way. "Jesus saith unto him, 'I am the way, the truth, and the life: no man cometh unto the Father, but by me'" (John 14:6).

I AM the Vine. "I am the vine, ye are the branches: He that abideth in me, and I in him, the same bringeth forth much fruit: for without me ye can do nothing" (John 15:5).

As noted previously, seven of the eight "I AM" statements have the construction, *"ego eimi"*, reflecting the Greek text of Exodus 3:14. "And God said unto Moses, 'I AM THAT I AM,' and he said, 'Thus shalt thou say unto the children of Israel, I AM hath sent me unto you.'"

In John 8:58, the words are at the end of the statement. "Jesus said unto them, 'Verily, verily, I say unto you, before Abraham was, I am.'" What provoked the Lord's statement about Abraham is provided in the context. "Then said Jesus to those Jews which believed on him, 'If ye continue in my word, then are ye my disciples indeed; and ye shall know the truth, and the truth shall make you free'" (John 8:31).

The word for, "shall make," [*eleuthero* (el-yoo-ther–o–o)], means, "to liberate." It can be translated, "deliver."

To continue, to abide in the Word of Jesus, brings knowledge of the truth, and after that, deliverance. For those who did not believe in Jesus, His words were insulting and inflammatory. "They answered him, 'We are Abraham's seed, and were never in bondage to any man: how sayest thou, "Ye shall be made free?"'" (John 8:33).

The Jews did not like to hear the word free, as if they were slaves. They viewed themselves as the chosen people of God, the children of Abraham, and therefore, in bondage to no one, not even Rome.

The practical problem that can immediately be seen, is that the Jews were either deliberately misunderstanding Jesus, or they were ignorant of spiritual matters. Jesus was not talking about physical bondage, social bondage, or military bondage. The Lord was talking about spiritual bondage. Those who are in bondage to sin must abide in Him and His teachings, if they want to know the truth, and find deliverance from the power and pollution of sin.

Since the Jews appealed to Abraham to deny they had any need of liberation, Jesus said something amazing. Jesus said He knew Abraham. In fact, before Abraham existed, Jesus existed. "Jesus answered them, 'Verily, verily, I say unto you, whosoever committeth sin is the servant of sin. And the servant abideth not in the house for ever: but the Son abideth ever. If the Son therefore shall make you free, ye shall be free indeed'" (John 8:34–36). "Jesus said unto them, 'Verily, verily, I say unto you, before Abraham was, I am'" (John 8:58).

In response to His critics, the Lord redirects their attention to the spiritual message He would have them hear. The Lord would teach that those who practice sin become the slaves of sin. Sin is personified, and presented as a severe taskmaster who keeps subjects in bondage. There is an irony in the dialogue of Jesus with the Jews of His day. It is possible for people to be in a form of slavery, and not even realize it. That is a problem in theology. People can be in a form of bondage in the sight of God, and not even know it.

For example, Pelagius, the fifth-century British monk, taught the free will of man. However, his definition of freedom was very expansive. Pelagius taught that a person was free to be greater than they were by nature. Pelagius believed that a person is free to be different by an exercise of their will. Pelagius would give an affirmative answer to Jeremiah's question about change, despite the divine interpretation. "Can the Ethiopian change his skin, or the leopard his spots? Then may ye also do good, that are accustomed to do evil" (Jeremiah 13:23).

Augustine taught that man had a free will, too, but it was very restricted. Augustine taught that a person can only act consistently with their will, but not contrary to it. Since the will of the natural man is bound to sin, a person is free to sin, but not free to please God. "So then they that are in the flesh cannot please God" (Romans 8:8). Both Pelagius and Augustine believed in free will.

No one can argue that people make choices, which is why there is trouble with God. We make choices that reflect our sinful passions and desires. At the same time we exercise our free will, we are also enslaved, according to Scripture. "For we ourselves also were sometimes foolish, disobedient, deceived, serving divers lusts and pleasures, living in malice and envy, hateful, and hating one another" (Titus 3:3).

What Augustine correctly pointed out, is that people do not have royal liberty. People are not free from themselves. People are not free from their own sinfulness. People are slaves to sinful impulses. People are not free to act contrary to their nature. They need a new nature. They need to be born again. The Humanist view of free will is that man is free from coercion, and man's will is indifferent. It has no predisposition, or inclination, bias, or bent toward sin. What is denied is the radical character of the Fall. The Jewish leaders did not want to hear about slavery, especially about slavery to sin. Sin reigns in the mortal body.

Here is the good news. A slave does not have to remain in a house forever. A slave can be made free. Jesus promises He can make individuals free from the

The Eighth "I AM"

reigning power of sin. "If the Son therefore shall make you free, ye shall be free indeed" (John 8:36).

"Lord, when?" "When will you make a slave free?" The answer is, "When a slave abides in my word, He becomes My disciple, and, if he continues in My word, then I shall make Him free." "Then said Jesus to those Jews which believed on him, 'If ye continue in my word, then are ye my disciples indeed'" (John 8:31).

> "There's a peace in my heart that the world never gave,
> A peace it cannot take away;
> Though the trials of life may surround like a cloud,
> I've a peace that has come here to stay!
>
> Constantly abiding, Jesus is mine;
> Constantly abiding, rapture divine;
> He never leaves me lonely, whispers, O so kind:
> "I will never leave thee," Jesus is mine.
>
> All the world seemed to sing of a Savior and King,
> When peace sweetly came to my heart;

Troubles all fled away and my night turned to day,
Blessed Jesus, how glorious Thou art!

This treasure I have in a temple of clay,
While here on His footstool I roam;
But He's coming to take me some glorious day,
Over there to my heavenly home!"[5]

"Let your conversation be without covetousness; and be content with such things as ye have: for he hath said, I will never leave thee, nor forsake thee" (Hebrews 13:5).

Jesus knew that His words to the Jewish leaders was not going to be received. In fact, Jesus knew they would seek to kill him. "I know that ye are Abraham's seed; but ye seek to kill me, because my word hath no place in you. I speak that which I have seen with my Father: and ye do that which ye have seen with your father" (John 8:37).

Notice that Jesus refers to the father of the Jewish leaders as being distinct from His Father. Again, the Jewish leaders did not understand. They did not discern that Jesus was saying that the devil was their

---

[5] Anne S. Murphy

The Eighth "I AM"

father. So they said, "Abraham is our father." "They answered and said unto him, 'Abraham is our father.' Jesus saith unto them, 'If ye were Abraham's children, ye would do the works of Abraham. But now ye seek to kill me, a man that hath told you the truth, which I have heard of God: this did not Abraham'" (John 8:39).

Once more Jesus had to clarify a spiritual truth to the Jewish leaders. If they were really the children of Abraham, they would do the works of Abraham. Specifically, they would receive the teachings of Jesus, and become His disciples. They would love Christ. "Jesus said unto them, 'If God were your Father, ye would love me: for I proceeded forth and came from God; neither came I of myself, but he sent me. Why do ye not understand my speech? Even because ye cannot hear my word. Ye are of your father the devil, and the lusts of your father ye will do. He was a murderer from the beginning, and abode not in the truth, because there is no truth in him. When he speaketh a lie, he speaketh of his own: for he is a liar, and the father of it'" (John 8:42).

One reason why the natural men, represented by the Jewish leaders, do not understand the words of Jesus, is because they do not take the time to listen.

The natural man will not listen to Christ because the natural man has the nature of his spiritual father, the devil. Because the natural man has the nature of his spiritual father, the devil, all of the natural desires of the devil will be performed.

By nature we are children of wrath. "Among whom also we all had our conversation in times past in the lusts of our flesh, fulfilling the desires of the flesh and of the mind; and were by nature the children of wrath, even as others" (Ephesians 2:3).

By nature we are children of disobedience. "Wherein in time past ye walked according to the course of this world, according to the prince of the power of the air, the spirit that now worketh in the children of disobedience" (Ephesians 2:2).

By nature we are children of the enemy of God. "Ye are of your father the devil, and the lusts of your father ye will do. He was a murderer from the beginning, and abode not in the truth, because there is no truth in him. When he speaketh a lie, he speaketh of his own: for he is a liar, and the father of it" (John 8:44).

The only way to become a child of God is through the new birth, and placed in a state of adoption. "There was a man of the Pharisees, named

The Eighth "I AM"

Nicodemus, a ruler of the Jews. The same came to Jesus by night, and said unto him, 'Rabbi, we know that thou art a teacher come from God: for no man can do these miracles that thou doest, except God be with him.' Jesus answered and said unto him, 'Verily, verily, I say unto thee, except a man be born again, he cannot see the kingdom of God'" (John 3:1–3). "For ye have not received the spirit of bondage again to fear; but ye have received the Spirit of adoption, whereby we cry, 'Abba, Father'" (Romans 8:15).

Secular society believes that as long as a person believes in God the Father, it does not matter what you believe. That is not true. To reject the Son, is to reject the Father who sent Him, who declared Him, and who vindicated Him by raising Him from the dead. "Let not your heart be troubled: ye believe in God, believe also in me" (John 14:1).

There is a motif throughout Scripture that Sonship is not measured by biology exclusively, but by faith, and obedience.

Children by faith. "For ye are all the children of God by faith in Christ Jesus" (Galatians 3:26).

Children by obedience. "By this we know that we love the children of God, when we love God, and keep his commandments" (1 John 5:2).

Listening to Christ, faith in Christ, and gospel obedience, will produce love in the heart for Jesus. Part of the judgment God gives to sinful people is to plug their ears, and to put scales over their eyes.

"For this people's heart is waxed gross, and their ears are dull of hearing, and their eyes they have closed; lest at any time they should see with their eyes, and hear with their ears, and should understand with their heart, and should be converted, and I should heal them" (Matthew 13:15).

"He hath blinded their eyes, and hardened their heart; that they should not see with their eyes, nor understand with their heart, and be converted, and I should heal them" (John 12:40).

"For the heart of this people is waxed gross, and their ears are dull of hearing, and their eyes have they closed; lest they should see with their eyes, and hear with their ears, and understand with their heart, and should be converted, and I should heal them" (Acts 28:27).

Only, when God, in His grace, removes the spiritual obstacles will people hear, see, believe, understand, and obey. If the world is correct, and the will must be indifferent and unbiased, then as a Christian, it must be said, that no one is free, for the will of the natural man is not unbiased, it is not indifferent, it is inclined to evil. The passionate desire of the natural man is to do the will of their father, the devil.

The devil does not force or compel a person to do the will of Satan. It is deeper than that. People want to do the will of the devil. Most frightening of all, Jesus said, "Ye will do the work of the devil." People want to do evil, and they will do evil. "Ye are of your father the devil, and the lusts of your father ye will do. He was a murderer from the beginning, and abode not in the truth, because there is no truth in him. When he speaketh a lie, he speaketh of his own: for he is a liar, and the father of it. And because I tell you the truth, ye believe me not" (John 8:44).

Having told the Jewish leaders they were not of their father Abraham, but of their father the devil, having told them they want to sin, and will do evil, Jesus challenged them to step forward, and convict Him of sin. They have sin, but where is the charge of sin, that is valid, against Him? "Which of you convinceth me of sin? And if I say the truth, why do ye not believe me?" (John 8:46).

The Jewish leaders could not accuse Jesus of sin, nor could they believe in Jesus, because they were not of God. Jesus does not say the people could not hear because they were stupid or uninformed. They could not hear, because they were not of God. "He that is of God heareth God's words: ye therefore hear them not, because ye are not of God" (John 8:47).

Upon hearing such plain charges against them, the Jews exploded in anger. "Then answered the Jews, and said unto him, 'Say we not well that thou art a Samaritan, and hast a devil?'" (John 8:48–53).

Jesus denied He had a demon, and offered eternal life to those who believed in Him. "Jesus answered, 'I have not a devil; but I honour my Father, and ye do dishonour me. And I seek not mine own glory: there is one that seeketh and judgeth. Verily, verily, I say unto you, If a man keep my saying, he shall never see death'" (John 8:49).

The woman of Samaria asked Jesus if He was greater than Jacob, who gave the well. Here, the Jews ask if Jesus was greater than Abraham.

Greater than Jacob. "The woman saith unto him, 'Sir, thou hast nothing to draw with, and the well is deep: from whence then hast thou that living water? Art thou greater than our father Jacob, which gave us the well, and drank thereof himself, and his children, and his cattle?'" (John 4:11).

The Eighth "I AM"

Greater than Abraham. "Then said the Jews unto him, 'Now we know that thou hast a devil. Abraham is dead, and the prophets; and thou sayest, "If a man keep my saying, he shall never taste of death." Art thou greater than our father Abraham, which is dead? And the prophets are dead: whom makest thou thyself?'" (John 8:52).

To a sarcastic question, Jesus answered honestly. "Jesus answered, 'If I honour myself, my honour is nothing: it is my Father that honoureth me; of whom ye say, that he is your God: yet ye have not known him; but I know him: and if I should say, I know him not, I shall be a liar like unto you: but I know him, and keep his saying. Your father Abraham rejoiced to see my day: and he saw it, and was glad. Then said the Jews unto him, 'Thou art not yet fifty years old, and hast thou seen Abraham?' Jesus said unto them, 'Verily, verily, I say unto you, before Abraham was, I am'" (John 8:54–58).

Jesus did not say, "Before Abraham was, I was." Rather, Jesus spoke of His eternal existence. Jesus is the eternal, "I AM." He was before Abraham.

When Abraham was promised to be the father of the seed of the Messiah, the patriarch believed God, and was justified. Abraham was being told about

Christ. Since he rejoiced about Christ, the Jews to whom Jesus spoke should be rejoicing that He was in their midst. Jesus is the Logos, the pre-existent, eternal One.

The Jews did not miss what Jesus was saying. They understood His claim to deity. They wanted to kill Him for such a claim. "Then they took up stones to cast at him: but Jesus hid himself, and went out of the temple, going through the midst of them, and so passed by" (John 8:59).

Their opposition was to no avail. Jesus remains the great I AM.

www.ingramcontent.com/pod-product-compliance
Lightning Source LLC
Chambersburg PA
CBHW061439040426
42450CB00007B/1132